YAZ

Carl Yastrzemski with Al Hirshberg

NEW YORK · THE VIKING PRESS

To Carol, Maryann, Mike, and Suzann

CONTENTS

Illustrations follow page 88

YAZ

CHAPTER 1

The Impossible Dream Come True

We had just beaten the Minnesota Twins to pull into a tie with them for first place on the next-to-last day of the 1967 season, but you'd think we had clinched the pennant. It was a wild, mad night—a night of happiness and apprehension; a night of hope and fear; a night of crazy-quilt colors, of blues and reds and whites and yellows and greens and blacks and purples all mixed up; a night of people, people of goodwill, crowding against bars and tables and each other, talking baseball, and drinking and eating and smoking and calling out my name; a night of absurd contrasts that found me restless yet contented, nervous yet relaxed, confident yet scared; a night of family intimacy in an atmosphere of public adulation; a night of relatives and friends; a night so confusing that no detail should be sharp in my mind, for it should all be lost in the delirium of the whole. Yet I can remember everything as though it happened yesterday, and I'm sure I'll remember everything till the day I die.

There was my wife, Carol, and our two older children, Maryann and Mike, and my parents from Bridgehampton, Long Island, and my brother Rich; and my uncle Mike Skonieczny and his wife, Theresa; and my uncle Jerry Skonieczny and his wife, Bert; and my uncle John Skonieczny and his wife, Helen; and my uncle Ray Yastrzemski and his wife, Dot; and my cousin Stan Yastrzemski, who once played football for Harvard; and Carol's parents from Pittsburgh, Mr. and Mrs. Walter Casper, and Carol's brother, Walter Casper, Jr., and his wife; and the Bill McNamaras and the Tony Tiskas and the Dan Gallaghers and the Paul Procopios and the Dr. Richard Wrights and their son, Edward, escorting Carol's sister, Suzanne—all of us having dinner at Stella's, in Boston's North End, as guests of Louis and Charlie Polcari, who own the place.

It was jammed with Red Sox fans, most of whom, I guess, had seen the Red Sox beat the Twins 6–4 that afternoon to go into a top tie with them for the leadership of the American League. They had seen me get three hits, including my 44th home run, to carry on a streak of personal heroics so unusual that Joe Garagiola had once said to me, "Hey, Superman, when do you jump off the top of the Empire State Building and float down to the street on the wings of your cape?" They had followed us through a dream season that had made us the darlings of baseball fans everywhere, for we were underdogs of the most hopeless variety—a ball club which had finished ninth in 1966, half a game from the cellar, and which had been a 100-to-1 shot to win the pennant when the season began. They had seen us in the thick of a fantastic four-club battle in which we had played musical chairs between first and fourth places with the Twins, the Chicago White Sox, and the Detroit Tigers almost all through the last half of the season.

Now, on this noisy Saturday evening at Stella's, we were one night away from a possible pennant. The Twins were in town for the final game of the year. The White Sox were out of the race, but the Tigers, half a game behind us, still had a chance. While we and the Twins were meeting in the most important single game of the year, they were playing the California Angels in a doubleheader at Detroit and could force a playoff by winning both games.

All around me people were discussing the possibilities in this wildest of all pennant races: "If the Twins win, we're out of it." . . . "If we beat the Twins and the Tigers split, we're in." . . . "If we beat the Twins and the Tigers win both, we have a playoff with the Tigers." . . . People of all ages were telling each other and telling me, and I was grinning and nodding in agreement. We were all talking about percentages, who would be where if what happened, how it might happen. And whenever I was asked, which was maybe a million times, I said, "Yes, yes, sure—we'll beat 'em tomorrow."

In all the talk that came from every direction at Stella's that night, the motif seemed to be me. I knew, for everywhere I turned I heard, "Yaz . . ." "Yaz . . ." "Yaz . . ." "If Yaz has a good day . . ." "Yaz can win it. . . ." "Yaz has come through in every clutch. . . ." It was flattering and sweet to my ears, except that I knew it wasn't Yaz alone. The Red Sox had made it to here as a team, and Yaz was part of that team. Yaz could have his greatest year, but no pennant would land in Boston unless everyone else did his part. Yaz didn't get us where we were. He only helped. So did everyone else—Manager Dick Williams and Jim Lonborg and George Scott and Rico Petrocelli and Tony Conigliaro and all the rest. But that night in Stella's they talked about me, maybe because I was there, and, as I ate my steak, I felt warm and good and sure of myself. Naturally we would win tomorrow. Naturally the Tigers would do no better than split. And naturally that would mean the pennant for us—the first Red Sox pennant and the first pennant for owner Tom Yawkey in twenty-one years. I sat there for a couple of hours, signing autographs and telling everyone not to worry, assuring them that we weren't going to lose after having come this far.

Between autographs and handshakes and happy fragments of conversation, I looked around the table and glowed at the sight of those closest to me: my wife, my children, my parents, my brother, my other relatives, my friends. Yet sometimes I felt a slight, quick pang of sadness that my grandfather Skonieczny couldn't be there. This was a moment he would have enjoyed, just as he would have enjoyed so many of the wonderful moments I had enjoyed during the season. Although many years had gone by since his death, the thought of him flashed across my mind more often than anyone knew, perhaps more often than I knew myself. It was never a long, sustained thought, just a flash of a second or so. But that was enough. There was so much to think about, for Grandpa Skonieczny and I had understood each other as only a man and a small boy together every day could understand each other. We had a very special relationship that put us in a world of our own. Close as my parents were to me, even they were not part of that world. It could exist only for Grandpa Skonieczny and me. And, with all that went on that night at Stella's, there was still room in my thoughts for this warm man who had left us too soon.

As the night wore on, the crowd grew, the talk became louder and the demand for autographs greater. When it was time to go, Louis Polcari came over and said, "You can't leave by the front door. There must be five hundred people there. They'll never let you through. Take your family and follow us out through the kitchen."

So, like thieves in the night, Carol and Maryann and Mike and I sneaked out through the kitchen into a car in the back alley and were driven to the Boston Harbor Police Station on Atlantic Avenue, where we had left our own car. Until I got behind the wheel, I had been buoyed up by sheer happiness, but as we drove the children home to Lynnfield I suddenly suffered a complete letdown, a deep depression, a reaction from all the excitement. My nerves were jumping so much that I wanted to stop the car, get out, and run myself to exhaustion. After we dropped the children off, Carol and I went to the nearby Colonial Statler Hilton Inn, where we were spending the night. Everybody was going to meet us there, but I didn't want to do any more partying, even though it was only about ten o'clock. While Carol went out to make apologies for me, I holed up in our room with the Sunday papers to quiet my nerves. After reading all about the game that afternoon, I put out the lights and tried to sleep.

Although I often drop off in a few seconds for a nap just before a ball game, I usually toss around half an hour or so before going to sleep at night. This time, with my stomach churning and my nerves jangling, I turned back and forth in bed for hours. At first I played and replayed Saturday's game with its happy ending, but instead of lulling me to sleep it woke me up more, and pretty soon I was worrying about Sunday's game.

Everybody's depending on me. . . . What if I flop? . . . What if Dean Chance stops me cold? . . . What if I don't get a hit off him? . . . What if I come up with the winning run on base and strike out or pop up or something? . . . Or if it's the tying run and it costs us the ball game? . . . They all say Yaz this and Yaz that, but what happens if Yaz dies on them? . . . How much can they expect? . . . Do they really think, like Garagiola, that I'm Superman, that I can do anything? . . . I'm human, I can make mistakes. . . . What if I pull a rock, make an error that costs us runs? . . . I've been a hero all season, but maybe tomorrow I'll be a goat. . . . Then they'll remember me all right. . . . Yaz, the guy who lost the pennant by dropping a fly ball or throwing to the wrong base or something. . . . Some hero I'll be then. . . . They'll boo me out of the ball park. . . .

I don't think I even dozed for hours. I remember hearing a clock somewhere strike three—the same clock I had heard striking midnight and one and two. When I finally went to sleep, it was not a deep sleep but a troubled, exhausting one in which I must have tossed around as much as before. I awoke at six, my stomach still churning, my nerves still jangling, and I got out of bed with the horrible feeling that this was going to be a bad day for everyone.

I'm scared. . . . Good Lord, I'm scared. . . . It's all up to me and I'm frightened to death. . . . We're not going to make it. . . . We'll lose the pennant as sure as I'm standing here. . . . How can we win? . . . The Twins are a better ball club.

. . . Chance is a great pitcher, maybe better than Lonborg . . . Killebrew is a great hitter, better than I am. . . . We can't win today. . . . We're going to lose. . . . This whole thing is a crazy dream. . . . We did well to get this far. . . . We won't go the rest of the way. . . . We have no right being where we are. . . . We'll lose . . . we'll lose . . . we'll lose . . .

I dressed quickly and was just leaving the room when Carol woke up. "Where are you going?"

"Out for a walk."

"A walk?"

"Yes."

"Are you all right?"

"Yes, I'm fine," I said. "Go back to sleep."

Dressed in light slacks and a sport coat, I stepped out into the cold October dawn and went quickly up to the golf clubhouse, then walked a couple of holes before turning back. By then, although the sun had come up, I was freezing, but I didn't want to go back to the inn. I was hungry, too, but the restaurant wouldn't be open until eight, which meant I had an hour to kill. I decided to kill it driving my car somewhere.

I got into it, turned on the motor and the heater, and started north on Route 128, the big belt superhighway that circles Boston, meeting every major road leading into the city. I went all the way to Gloucester, into the town and around some of the narrow, winding streets, then headed back to the Colonial. I got there at eight, just as the restaurant opened.

I felt terrible, lethargic and dopey and disheartened. My head ached from lack of sleep, and, even though I had been hungry, I couldn't eat all the steak and eggs I ordered for breakfast. Usually on the morning of a game I think about the pitcher I'm going to face—what he has, how he pitches me, how he's likely to pitch me that day, if I can outguess him—but I couldn't concentrate.

I haven't had enough sleep. . . . Chance will kill me. . . . I won't be able to hit him today. . . . I won't be able to hit anybody. . . . I won't react properly to anything. . . . I can't even eat right. . . . I feel lousy. . . . In six hours I'll play the most important game of my life and not be able to do anything. . . . What am I going to do? . . . What can I do? . . . I've got to get organized. . . . I can't play a ball game feeling like this. . . . I'll go 0 for 4. . . .

I drove into town alone and worried all the way. I couldn't remember a day all season that I had felt worse facing a ball game. When I arrived at Fenway Park around ten-thirty, I was really upset, but I tried not to show it.

"How are you feeling, Yaz?" Don Fitzpatrick, the equipment manager and my best friend in the Red Sox locker room, was grinning at me.

"Fine," I said.

"Well, go get 'em," he said. "Here—some things for you to sign."

After I dressed, I signed maybe two dozen balls, half a dozen bats, and some pictures, then went out to the field to try batting practice. Usually I either bat or field to warm up before a game—rarely both. This time I thought maybe if I took some swings I could get rid of the dull, dead feeling that had plagued me all night, but it didn't work. I swung perhaps fifteen times and couldn't get the ball out of the infield. Irritated, more upset than ever, I walked to the dugout, put my bat in the rack, and went back to the locker room.

I signed more autographs, fooled around with odds and ends in my locker, and talked with Fitzie, but I felt no better when it was time to send Keith Rosenthal, the batboy, up to the press kitchen for some lunch. He left at exactly ten minutes to twelve, and returned with a steak, baked potato, and Jello and whipped cream at exactly noon. We had gone through this routine every day for weeks, doing everything the same at the same times, and it had brought us luck. Keith got me a Coke, and after eating everything I felt a little better. But I was still nervous and apprehensive when I went into the trainer's room to take my pregame nap on one of the tables there.

When Fitzie got me up at one-forty-five, fifteen minutes before game time, I was a little more rested, since I had slept well for half an hour or so. I jumped into a cold shower, then played catch with Jimmy Jackson, another batboy, throwing the ball the length of the locker room to loosen up. Before putting on my uniform I asked Buddy LeRoux, the trainer, to work on my legs, and he gave me a fast rub. I was dressed and in the dugout at one minute to two, just as Dick Williams and Manager Cal Ermer of the Twins were finishing the daily meeting about ground rules with the umpires at the plate.

As Williams returned to the dugout I ran out to my position in left field, then, after the National Anthem, I said a Hail Mary, as I always do.

Then, just as always, I prayed: "Please let me relax, and be with me, and let me play my natural game, to the best of my ability, and not be injured."

The Twins took a 1–0 lead in the first inning, during which nothing happened to make me feel any better. When I went to the plate to face Chance as the third man up in our half of the first inning, the bat felt like lead. He threw me a curve, which I let go by; then he came in with a fast sinker. I swung, badly, but hit the ball hard up the middle. Chance knocked it down but couldn't recover in time to throw me out, and I had an infield single, a cheap hit that didn't even feel good when I connected. Maybe I didn't have much else, but at least luck was with me.

When the inning ended, I ran hard to left field, going full speed from the dugout to the wall, trying to generate some circulation, to get my heart pumping, so I wouldn't feel so hopelessly dead. At the wall I turned back and started my usual game of catch with Reggie Smith, the center fielder. Ordinarily we just lob the ball back and forth to keep loose, but this time I threw overhand and hard, putting almost as much on the ball as I would have if I were trying to get a base-runner in a game. It helped a little, but I still didn't feel right, still couldn't shake the deadly physical and mental lethargy that had gripped me all day.

In the Twins' half of the third inning Cesar Tovar walked

with one out; then Harmon Killebrew hit a single along the ground through the hole between shortstop and third base. I could have played it safe, waiting for the ball to come to me, but Tovar is fast and I wanted to hold him to second base. I rushed in, charging the ball, intending to scoop it up with my glove hand, but it went right by me. It was clearly an error, and while I was chasing the ball back to the fence Tovar went all the way home with the Twins' second run of the game, giving them a 2–0 lead.

Oh, brother, I thought, *the fans will get on me now, and I can't think of anyone who deserves it more.* But the fans didn't get on me. There wasn't a single boo from the crowd in the left-field section of the grandstand—only yells of encouragement and even some applause. Bad as I felt—and now I was really down mentally—I appreciated their attitude, and as I ran in at the end of the inning I hoped that somehow I could make up for this ridiculous mistake which might cost us the pennant.

Chance was still pitching when I came up for the second time, to lead off our half of the third. The bat still didn't feel right as I got ready to hit. I took a practice swing and there was only the same dull ache in my arms, as though I had just set down a dead weight too heavy for me to lift in the first place. The Twins' pitcher threw a sinking fast ball over the plate, and I tried to pull it, which I shouldn't have, feeling the way I felt. The ball zipped off my bat, foul, and I stepped out of the box, knowing that luck had been with me again. If I had hit it fair, it would have dribbled weakly down to second.

I'm glad I fouled it off. . . . Even if it was in there, I should have let it go by. . . . I'm not going to belt one out of the park. . . . I've got to stop trying to pull. . . . Just meet the ball, that's all. . . . Go with the pitch. . . . Don't try to do anything with it. . . . If it's outside, hit it to left. . . . Otherwise, just try to go down the middle with it. . . .

I finished rubbing dirt on my hands, then moved back into the box, adjusting my sleeves, pushing my helmet firmly onto my head, reaching across the plate with the bat, making sure I was covering the strike zone. I shrugged once, dug in hard with my left foot, closed my stance a little, and looked down at Chance. He got his sign, stepped on the rubber, and reared back to pitch. As the ball left his hand I could see it was a curve—you can tell it by the spin—and I brought my bat around to meet it. The ball soared high to left, so high that at first I thought it was going out of the park for a home run, and I started jogging. Then, realizing that the wind would hold it back, I ran hard, rounded first, and, as the ball bounced off the wall, got into second with a stand-up double.

Now I was 2 for 2 and still didn't feel good. A scratch hit to the infield and a double off the wall are not a bad day's work for a hitter, but they gave me no joy, for the lethargy, the heaviness in my arms and my legs and my body hung on like a millstone. Perhaps if I had scored I might have pulled out of it, but I died on second base, and when I went to the outfield for the Twins' fourth we were still trailing 2–0.

Once again I threw hard as I played catch with Reggie, and once again I felt a little looser. I jumped up and down at my position for a few seconds, then got set for the inning. When it was over I ran full speed to the dugout, then moved around in it while we were hitting in the fourth. We didn't score, and neither did the Twins in their fifth, and the score was the same when we came up for our half of the inning. If one man reached, I'd get another shot at Chance before the fifth was over.

Jim Lonborg, leading off, caught the Twins' infield by surprise with a bunt down the third-base line that Tovar couldn't handle. Lonny beat it out for his second hit of the game and went to second when Jerry Adair slapped a base hit past second baseman Rod Carew. As Dalton Jones moved into the batter's box with two on and nobody out, the crowd began chanting, "Go—go—go," while I went from the dugout to the on-deck circle. As I walked toward it, hearing that "Go—go—go" in the background, I suddenly felt wonderful. I gripped the bat and swung it twice, and my wrists and arms were loose and the bat was like an extension of my hands, easy and natural and part of me.

My head was clear, the dull ache in my muscles gone, and gone too was the weight of the world that had rested for so long on my shoulders.

As Jones stood waiting for Chance's first pitch, I crouched in the on-deck circle. My eyes were on Chance leaning out for his sign, but—just for a flash, a fraction of a second—I didn't see him or anything in the ball park at all. I saw myself walking hand-in-hand with Grandpa Skonieczny toward the tractor in back of his house on the edge of the potato farm he worked in Bridgehampton. He picked me up and sat me on the tractor seat as we grinned at each other and talked idly of the things kids and their grandfathers talk about in the heat of a summer morning. The picture was gone almost as soon as it appeared, but it gave me an additional lift, and I knew that whatever I did in the moments to follow would, in my own mind, be in memory of my grandfather. It was almost as if he were crouching beside me in the on-deck circle there at Fenway Park in Boston on this last day of the baseball season, telling me in the accents of his native Poland that everything was going to be all right.

Jones fouled off a bunt attempt, then got the sign to hit away. As Tovar rushed in from third for another bunt, Jones hit one right past him into left field, and the bases were loaded with nobody out. I jumped up, tossed aside the heavy practice bat, and walked quickly toward the plate as Ermer came out to talk to Chance. The fans were screaming, but the noise sounded like background music and had the same effect on me, for it soothed my nerves and made me feel as though everyone in the ball park were as confident as I.

He's in a tough spot, his toughest of the game, and he'll challenge me with his best pitch. . . . He'd be crazy to do it any other way. . . . He'll throw me a hard sinker, low and away. . . . I mustn't try to pull it, just to hit it. . . . I'll close my stance, pull my rear in, face the guy and hit his pitch. . . . It won't go out of the ball park, but it will be a hit. . . . I know it will be a hit. . . . I know it . . . I know it . . .

The conference on the mound broke up, and I literally

bounced up to the plate. I never was so sure of myself in my life. As I dug in, now completely oblivious to the tremendous racket around me, I felt so good I didn't even take a practice swing. My bat was right, my hands were right, my fingers wrapped around the bat perfectly, and I had that power feeling which comes only with supreme, absolute confidence. When I was all ready, my stance closed, my rear in, my bat ready for the swing, I wanted to shout, *Come on, come on. Get the ball up here so I can hit it. The last time you threw me that sinker I was lucky and fouled it off instead of dribbling it to second. You'll throw it now and I'll hit it fair and safe. Throw it, throw it, get it up here. . . .*

With the bases full, Chance took a full wind-up, and threw a fast ball low and inside for a ball. *Next pitch, next pitch,* I thought. *It has to be the next pitch.* Chance took his sign, looked over at Lonborg on third base, wound up, and threw, and the minute he let the ball go I knew this time I was right. It was the sinker, low and on the outside corner, going to exactly the spot and at exactly the speed I expected. I didn't try to kill the ball or pull it. I just stepped into it, swinging easy but solidly. The ball shot on a line over second base, and in came Lonny and Adair with the runs that tied up the game.

That one was for Grandpa Skonieczny.

Before the inning was over we scored five runs, knocked Chance out of the box, and took a 5–2 lead, but we still had to get the Twins out in the next three innings. Although pitching well, Lonborg got into trouble in the eighth. With two out, Harmon Killebrew and Tony Oliva hit successive singles, bringing up Bob Allison. A hard-hitting right-hander, he's very dangerous in Fenway Park, with its left-field fence only 315 feet from the plate. It's not a hard field to play, but you have to get the hang of it. I practically lived out there from 1961 on, so I know every square inch of that wall, how a ball will bounce off it, which I can catch and which I have to play on the carom. An outfielder with a good arm can hold almost anything off there to a single, unless it's a high drive that takes so long to come down it gives the runner time to make it to second.

Tougher to play than the fence itself is the wall in front of the left-field grandstand, which runs along the foul line, at right angles to the fence. There's not much foul territory at that point, so the left fielder has no running room at all. Worse, you can't play too close to the line because even a dead pull hitter seldom hits one right on it. If he gets the ball into the corner where the grandstand fence meets the wall, it's a sure double, which, with two out and the base-runners moving as soon as the ball is hit, might score both of them if there's a fast man on first.

Even playing Allison to pull, I wasn't so close to the foul line that I could get over there easily. But sure enough, he hit one just inside the line, headed for the corner. If it got by, it was a two-run double, which would cut our lead to 5–4 and put the tying run on second. I started over there as Allison hit the ball, and must have got a tremendous jump, because I managed to backhand it and keep it out of that deadly corner.

From there on I did everything by instinct, for all I remember is seeing, out of the corner of my eye, Allison rounding first base. Only on later reflection could I explain what my thinking must have been. Certainly there was a question of where to throw the ball, and how. I was off balance, but close enough to the grandstand wall to brace my foot against it if I threw to second. Ordinarily the natural move would have been to throw home. I couldn't keep Killebrew from scoring, but I might get Oliva. However, he's very fast, and I could see him approaching third as I grabbed the ball. By the time I got set to throw he would be around the bag and on his way to the plate, and I wouldn't have the benefit of pushing off the wall with my foot if I threw in that direction. At best, it would take a perfect throw, and the play would be very close.

There was one other factor. Allison is a slow runner who normally would have no reason to hustle to second, since he would figure that I'd throw home. When I picked him up he had just crossed first base, and I knew he couldn't possibly beat a good throw to second. So, planting my foot firmly against the wall, I shot the ball on a line and got Allison by twenty feet. It was probably the best and certainly the most important throw I made all year. It got us out of the inning still two runs ahead, and left the Twins with their power used up and only one inning to go.

Fifteen minutes later it was all over. When Rich Rollins, the Twins' pinch-hitter, popped up to Rico Petrocelli, I ran toward short and was right behind him as he caught the ball for the last out of the game. The two of us jumped about ten feet straight up in the air, and I swerved toward Lonny. But the crowd was spilling out of the stands and beginning to sweep over the field, blocking the way to the dugout behind first base, so I took a big right turn and sprinted for the backstop, then worked my way to the dugout from that direction. Everybody was wildly happy, and I screamed and yelled along with the rest. As I fought my way through the crowd I was pawed from every direction and I must have been clobbered by half a dozen flying elbows. One got me right in the jaw, and when I finally reached the dugout steps I was still trying to shake off the effects of the blow.

I ran the length of the runway, took the clubhouse steps two and three at a time, and was the first ballplayer into the locker room. There Ken Coleman, our regular announcer, and Don Gillis of Station WHDH in Boston shoved microphones in front of me, and pretty soon lights were flashing and cameras were grinding and people were yelling back and forth and guys were squirting each other with shaving cream, beer, and soda pop, and writers and cameramen and radio and television people were all over the place.

As the ballplayers trooped in, we started shoving each other in and out of the showers, uniforms and all. I was standing, dripping from head to foot, water even squishing out of my shoes, when Joe Foy, an unlighted cigar in his mouth, came toward me. As we squirted each other with shaving cream and beer— there wasn't champagne, because we hadn't clinched the pennant yet—somebody yelled, "Hey, Joe, give Yaz the cigar."

Foy lit the cigar and passed it over to me, and I kept it in my mouth long enough for pictures, then took it out because I'm not much of a smoker.

The interviews began as everyone kept pouring stuff over everyone else, and it wasn't long before the floor had a film of beer and soda pop on it.

Lonny came in looking like the wrath of God. He had been swept all the way out to left field by the delirious crowd, and it took him twenty minutes to get back. His uniform was torn to shreds. From the waist up, all he wore was bracelets of his undershirt around his wrists, but he didn't mind. He had a huge grin on his face as he took a position around the corner from me, with the reporters and everyone else moving back and forth between us.

I got up on a chair in front of my locker to answer questions from writers standing ten deep in front of me. Microphones kept getting shoved into my face, and I didn't have the slightest idea whom they belonged to or where my voice was being carried. The same questions came over and over: "How did you stand the pressure?" . . . "What kept you going?" . . . "How could you run and throw and field and hit the way you did?" . . . "What kind of pitches did you hit?" Guys kept pointing out that I had finished the season with six straight hits—I got my fourth of the game off Jim Roland after Chance had been knocked out of the box—and that I had won the triple crown, leading the league in batting and runs batted in and tying with Killebrew for the home-run lead, and people asked me about that.

Tony Conigliaro, one of the best young right-handed hitters in baseball, who had been knocked out for the season by a pitch that hit him in the eye six weeks earlier, came over in the midst of the interviews. He shook my hand and said, his voice shaking, "Yaz, this is the greatest year that any ballplayer ever had. I knew every time a situation arose, you would deliver. I don't know how you did it." Then he moved away, and I heard later that he broke down and cried, for his inability to play was a terrible blow to him. But he had already done his part before being hurt. If it hadn't been for him, we wouldn't have been in contention at all.

Somebody brought Lonny over beside me, and the two of us just looked at each other and bubbled over—both soaking wet, our hair matted with beer and soda and shaving cream. We grabbed each other and kept yelling, "Great—great—great . . ." and tried to answer questions together. Reggie Smith walked by, and I made him join us. Then Petrocelli came along, and the four of us posed for pictures, the messiest-looking quartet of saturated ballplayers you ever saw.

Over in the far corner of the room, at the door opposite Dick Williams' office, I suddenly saw my dad, beaming with pride and joy as he stood with two of my uncles, Mike and John Skonieczny. I wanted to go over and embrace him, for I knew that this was the culmination of all his dreams, the result of all his patience, the answer to all his prayers. I was the ballplayer he had wanted to be and might have become if he hadn't had to work so hard on the potato farm. He had coached me from babyhood, had taught me all the early baseball lessons I ever learned, had helped me even after I became a professional, and had given me the encouragement and inspiration I needed to travel the road that had led to this soul-satisfying climax.

With people pressing in all around me, I couldn't go to him, and I'm sure he didn't want me to. All he wanted was to stand and quietly savor the moment, perhaps the greatest moment of his life as well as of mine. When I caught his eye and smiled and raised an arm in greeting, he smiled back and nodded, as if to say, "Nice going, son," and when I turned away such a glow of happiness engulfed me that for a few seconds I found it hard to utter a word. Whenever I looked over at this slight blue-eyed man to whom I owed so much, I had the same feeling, as I'm sure he did. The smile never left his face, and I guess his eyes never left me.

Dick O'Connell, the Red Sox general manager, and Haywood Sullivan, the player personnel director, came in, waving and grinning and slapping people on the back. By now the writers must have been twenty deep, and the questions—the same questions as before—were still coming thick and fast. Then, behind the writers, standing close to the opposite wall and not far from my dad, I spotted Mr. Yawkey. He was smiling and one hand was raised in triumph, as he formed with his lips the words, "I'll see you when you finish."

When the crowd broke, I beckoned to my father and, after greeting him, introduced him to Mr. Yawkey, who invited him to join a party in his private suite. I was still soaked, but Mr. Yawkey put his arms around me and we squeezed each other in a bear hug, and he said in a choking voice, "I don't know how to thank you."

"Don't try," I said. "I just hope that this makes up for some of the things you've done for me and my family over the past six years, and that it helps a little in making you and Mrs. Yawkey happy."

"It sure does," Mr. Yawkey said.

"It's been a long time," I said. "You and I are the only ones left who know what this actually means. We went through the bad years from nineteen sixty-one together."

"That's right," Mr. Yawkey said. "You're the last survivor of the nineteen sixty-one team, the oldest man on the ball club in point of service. You lived through the worst and now"—he spread his arms wide "—this."

I looked at him and said, "I got your clothes all wet, Mr. Yawkey."

"Never mind my clothes," he said. "The pennant is more important. I've waited a long time for this."

We all had to wait just a little longer. The Tigers, who had won the first game of their doubleheader with the Angels in Detroit, had already started the second. If they won that, they would tie us at the top and we'd be in a playoff. They got off to an early lead, but the Angels came back for three runs in the third to go in front, 4–3. We were getting the game direct from Tiger Stadium by radio, but we didn't pick up interest in it until then.

YAZ

As the noise in the locker room died down, the ballplayers began congregating around the radio near my locker. And as the game progressed, the writers and broadcasters and photographers and all the others crowded into the room backed off until the players were together in a semicircle and the others were out on the perimeter. There was no design, no pattern, no plan to this arrangement. It just happened, as though everyone knew instinctively that the team belonged together in these most important moments of the season, just as it had been together all year.

Somebody brought in a big box of sandwiches, and we nibbled on them, washing them down with Coke or water. The beer and soda pop were mostly on the floor, and there was nothing else to drink. We sat quietly, munching our sandwiches, drinking our Cokes, and not saying much. When Roger Repoz hit a two-run triple in the fourth to give the Angels a 7–3 lead, one of the guys said, "This is it, we're in," and a murmur went through our semicircle like a massive sigh. But mostly we were quiet, eating and drinking while we listened.

Later in the game somebody said, "I'm glad it's the Angels. Rigney won't give the Tigers an inch." Manager Bill Rigney of the Angels is that way—he'd fight for this ball game as though it would be his pennant, not ours, if he won. When the Tigers scored a couple of runs with two out in the seventh, he yanked Jim McGlothlin for Minnie Rojas, who got out of the inning with the Angels leading 8–5. When the Tigers came up in the last half of the ninth still trailing 8–5, the room was dead quiet. Everyone on the Red Sox team—players, coaches, and Manager Dick Williams, who had been upstairs at Mr. Yawkey's party—was huddled around the little radio in the locker room, listening to every pitch.

Bill Freehan led off for the Tigers with a double, and I thought, *My God, Detroit's going to win it. It's fate, Freehan leading off like that. They're going to rally.* The announcer said, "Weaver's in the bullpen," and I said aloud, "No, not Weaver. What's he doing in the bullpen? Get Brunet ready." A minute later the announcer said, "It's a mistake. It's Brunet warming up, not Weaver." A couple of guys cheered, and I said, "Bring him in, Rig, bring him in. What the hell are you waiting for?" Rojas walked Don Wert, and Rigney didn't wait any longer. The announcer said, "Rojas is out of there and Brunet's in." Referring to Tommy Ferguson, the Angels' traveling secretary, I yelled to Fitzie, "Call Fergie and tell him we'll give Brunet a year's supply of beer if he gets them out." And somebody yelled, "That'll cost you your World Series share." And I yelled back, "I don't care."

Then we were all quiet again as Brunet faced Jim Price, who was batting for Mickey Lolich. He hit a fly to Rich Reichardt in left, and somebody said, "That's one," and another murmuring sigh swept through the semicircle. Dick McAuliffe was up. The announcer said, "He hits one to Bobby Knoop at second," and I got set to jump, because Knoop and Jim Fregosi are maybe the best double-play combination in baseball. "He throws to Fregosi for one," the announcer said, "and Fregosi throws to first for two—" And that was all anybody heard, because we went nuts again in the locker room.

The next few minutes are a blur in my mind. I remember jumping high in the air, then, wet spikes and all, climbing up on a chair and yelling and yelling and yelling. Somebody produced champagne, now that we had the pennant wrapped up, and I got a stream of it right in the face. Fitzie had me around the ankles, telling me to get down before I got hurt, and when I finally did, it was right into somebody's arms. Everyone was hugging and kissing and pounding everyone else, and when a guy handed me an open bottle of champagne I stuck my finger in the neck of it and squirted it at random. There was champage flying all over the place; nobody was drinking it, we just squirted it. Dick Williams grabbed me, and we held on to each other, babbling and laughing. Then a guy yelled, "Yaz, make a speech," and I got pushed up on a table next to the water cooler.

When I looked around I noticed an odd thing. In all the confusion, the ballplayers were still together in the middle and the locker-room visitors still on the perimeter. This was our celebration. Nobody wanted to interfere, and nobody tried to. Here was one of the wild moments of baseball history, yet the writers and radio and TV people realized that it was our moment, not theirs. Only the cameramen were in action, but even they worked from a distance at first, respecting our obvious desire to stay together just a little longer.

I stood on the table, grinning and waving an empty bottle of champagne, and waited for the guys to quiet down. Then I said, "It's wonderful—it's wonderful. Thanks for a great year. Thanks for not quitting. Thanks for giving me the thrill of my life." Somebody hoisted Conigliaro up beside me; then Petrocelli came up, and Scott and Lonny and Foy and I don't know who else. All I know is that at one point there were eight ballplayers on that table and Fitzie was yelling, "Come down before somebody gets hurt. You guys have a World Series to play." Again he grabbed me by the ankles and helped me off the table. Then suddenly I realized my eyes were burning from the champagne shower, and I went in to wash them out. When I came out, things were a little calmer. Everybody was mingling with everybody else, and a mob of writers was at my locker waiting to talk to me.

Mr. Yawkey came over, and once again I soaked his suit as we embraced. There were tears in his eyes as he said over and over, "Thanks, thanks, thanks . . ." Dick Williams joined us, and we threw our arms around each other while microphones were shoved at us from all directions and still and movie cameras ground away and television lights half blinded us.

"When you're through here, come upstairs," Mr. Yawkey said. "The wives are waiting for you to join the party."

He moved away then, and I turned back for more interviews. I guess it was an hour after we clinched the pennant before things quieted down enough for me to start peeling off my sopping clothes so I could take a shower. I hadn't had a drop of beer or champagne to drink but I was high with joy and excitement, not caring whether school kept or not, not worrying or thinking about anything, living in a wonderful world of happiness because of this fantastic thing that had happened to us all.

I was still peeling off my clothes when Dick O'Connell, who had stayed in the background all through our double celebration, moved up beside me and said softly, "Yaz, you've got your six-figure contract for next year, and you deserve it."

He was so casual, so matter-of-fact, so quiet that for a few seconds I didn't get the full significance of what he said. When it hit me, all I could say was, "Thanks—thanks a million, Dick."

"Don't thank me," he said. "You earned it." Then, without another word, he turned and walked away.

Six figures: $100,000 a year, a huge salary for anybody, an unbelievable salary for the son of a potato farmer. The Red Sox locker room in Fenway Park in Boston, Massachusetts, at that moment of triumph seemed a million miles from Bridgehampton, Long Island, and I seemed a million years from my childhood there.

CHAPTER 2

Grandpa Skonieczny

Bridgehampton isn't on the way to anywhere except the tip of Long Island. Thirty miles southwest of Montauk Point and about a hundred miles from New York, it has a permanent population of some 3000, mostly of Polish, Italian, and Irish extraction, plus a small and exclusive community of wealthy summer residents who live in a world of shoreline mansions. The Poles —my people—are nearly all potato farmers. They work long, hard hours for a precarious living that makes nobody rich but rarely leaves anyone poor. Since they raise their own food, they never starve. My younger brother and I, surrounded by devoted relatives on both sides of the family, had a happy childhood. My father couldn't give me much money, but I didn't have to give him any either. I spent what I earned, ate well, had enough clothes to wear, including a new jacket at the beginning of each school year, and don't remember ever having been deprived of anything I needed or wanted badly.

I grew up in the six-room frame house on School Lane where my parents still live. I was close to my father's family, but I saw more of my mother's, since most of them lived in Bridgehampton and most of the Yastrzemskis lived in Water Mill, a few miles to the west. Until I was about ten years old, I saw Grandpa Skonieczny nearly every day of my life, far more often than I saw Grandpa Yastrzemski. Grandpa Skonieczny was tall and broad-shouldered, Grandpa Yastrzemski short and stocky, but except for appearance there was an amazing similarity between the two. Both came over from Poland at sixteen; both married Polish girls at eighteen; both had large families, all born in the Bridgehampton area; both were potato farmers; both got sick when I was about twelve (Grandpa Skonieczny with Parkinson's disease, and Grandpa Yastrzemski with bone cancer); and they died within three months of each other. They had not known each other in Poland, but they became good friends after my mother and father were married, and in the last years of their lives I frequently saw them together.

However vague early memories are, there is always someone or something that dominates them, and Grandpa Skonieczny and his livestock dominate mine. In the busy summer months my parents both worked; they left the house early and returned late. When I was very young Grandpa Skonieczny picked me up at about ten in the morning and, after buying me ice cream at the Candy Kitchen on the corner of our street and the Montauk Highway, took me to his farm on Mecox Road, about three miles south of our house. Sometimes my parents dropped me off there early, and we didn't go to the Candy Kitchen until late afternoon, when Grandpa Skonieczny took me home. My mother always thought the ice cream would ruin my appetite for supper, but it never did.

When I was old enough to have a bicycle, my parents and I raced each other to my grandparents' house every morning during the harvest season. They gave me a five-minute start, then followed me in the car with my younger brother, Rich. They usually beat me, but it was always close enough to be interesting. When we got a little older I took Rich on the bike, letting him ride on the handlebars.

I get a lump in my throat every time I visit my grandmother

in the farmhouse on Mecox Road, because it's so full of rich memories of Grandpa Skonieczny. She lives there with Uncle Mike and his family. The place looks much as it did while I was growing up. Most of the animals are gone, and so is the smokehouse. But the barn, now used principally as a garage, is still there, and the sandpit beside the smokehouse hasn't changed either. When my brother and I were small, we played there by the hour, making mudpies and castles and train tracks and things like that.

There were few things I enjoyed more than riding on the tractor beside Grandpa Skonieczny. He took me into the backyard, put me up on the seat, climbed up beside me, and off we'd go. When we got back we collected the afternoon eggs from the chicken house, then fed the poultry and the livestock. My particular job was feeding the pigs a mash made from peewee potatoes too small to market. We dumped the peewees into drums about a quarter full of water and stirred them over a fire until the mash was made.

My favorite animals were a huge billy goat and a baby calf. The goat was so big that I could ride him. Grandpa Skonieczny used to put me on his back and lead me around the yard, while I hung on by the horns. I adopted the calf the day he was born, and for seven weeks he and I were inseparable. The first thing I did when I reached the farm in the morning was go out and feed him. Then, with Grandpa Skonieczny walking beside me to make sure the calf didn't get skittish, I took him out to pasture, leading him by a chain. All day long I went back and forth from the yard to the pasture to see how my calf was doing and to nuzzle him, despite Grandpa Skonieczny's continual warnings not to touch him because he might suddenly buck or shy. At five in the afternoon Grandpa Skonieczny and I went out after him, and I led him back by the chain and got him ready for the night.

One day Grandpa Skonieczny said, "The calf is getting too big for you."

"He won't hurt me," I said.

"He has to go away anyhow," Grandpa Skonieczny said. "He's seven weeks old."

"Where is he going?"

"Just away," Grandpa Skonieczny said.

I burst into tears and said, "He's not just going away. You're going to call in the Polish DP."

Whenever they wanted an animal slaughtered, my grandfather or my uncles hired a big husky guy to come and do the job. I never knew his name, because the only way they referred to him was as the "Polish DP." I had no idea that "DP" meant "displaced person." I figured it had something to do with the man's occupation. All I knew about him was that whenever he came there'd be a slaughter, and I didn't want that happening to my calf.

Grandpa Skonieczny didn't deny that the Polish DP was coming, but he tried to soften the blow. "Your calf is going to heaven," he said.

I cried and cried, and when Grandpa Skonieczny took me in his arms I said, "You and Grandma and Uncle Mike and everybody are going to eat him, aren't you? Well, I'm not. I don't have to eat him, do I?"

"No, sonny," Grandpa Skonieczny said, "you don't have to eat him."

But I'm sure I did.

It never bothered me when grown animals were slaughtered—only when babies were. I could feed the chicks and the piglets and other young creatures and love them like pets, but when they grew up I didn't care what happened to them. I never saw livestock slaughtered, but I often watched Grandpa Skonieczny or Uncle Mike or my dad or somebody kill chickens in the back yard. They cut off the heads, and Grandpa Skonieczny and I used them for crab bait.

I guess I was eight or nine when Grandpa Skonieczny began taking me crabbing during the season. We left at about five in the afternoon and walked maybe half a mile to an inlet where there were plenty of crabs. Grandpa Skonieczny showed me how to tie the chicken head to a string and throw it out into the water. When a crab grabbed the head in its claws, you reeled the string in, just like a fishing line, pulled the crab off into a net, and threw the string out again. In a few hours you could get a bushel of crabs. We took them back to the farmhouse, where there was always somebody around—my parents and aunts and uncles—and my grandmother put them into a huge pot of boiling water so we could eat them on the spot. During the crabbing season we did this almost every night, including Saturdays, when we went early so we could get to the movies in Sag Harbor for the seven-o'clock show.

For years this was my biggest thrill. Sag Harbor is about ten miles north of us, and the trip over there became a ritual which lasted from the time I was five until I got out of high school. Grandpa Skonieczny wouldn't miss that Saturday-night movie with us for anything. Even after he got Parkinson's disease, which made him shake uncontrollably, he insisted on going to the seven-o'clock show Saturdays, just as we always had. Nobody cared about the picture; the thing that counted was to go. Until he was actually bedridden, Grandpa Skonieczny dragged himself off to the movies every single Saturday so we could all be together. From the day he died, neither my grandmother nor I ever set foot in that Sag Harbor theater again.

My grandmother was a wonderful cook. She made a Polish duck soup called czarnina, which I could eat by the gallon. Her other specialties were cabbage stuffed with ham or pork, called golompki, and plum dumplings, a marvelous combination of purple plums and potatoes. Unfortunately, purple plums are available only in summer, so now I miss them because I can't make it out to Bridgehampton at that time of the year, but I still get to eat her czarnina and her golompki from time to time. They taste as good to me today as they did twenty years ago.

She also concocted a delicious mushroom dish, made from mushrooms we picked ourselves. Sometimes we made an all-day excursion, leaving Bridgehampton early in the morning and driving to Montauk Beach, thirty miles away. She and Grandpa Skonieczny and I picked mushrooms for hours, then drove home to eat them. Once, I got deathly sick; the mushrooms were poisonous, but apparently only to me. They didn't affect either of my grandparents. I was in pretty bad shape for three days—so bad that I couldn't go home, and my parents slept over at Grandpa's. I guess nobody got much sleep. I learned later they thought I wouldn't make it. The doctor kept coming in and out, and all four of them, parents and grandparents, stayed up with me night after night until I was all right. I have not been very big for mushrooms since.

Another time Grandpa Skonieczny rushed me to the hospital after I crushed a toe when an iron ball fell on it. Uncle Mike, my mother's youngest brother, was a shot-putter on the school track team, and he kept his twelve-pound shot in the room where he slept. One day I picked it up and dropped it on my toe. While I yelled bloody murder, Grandpa Skonieczny scooped me up and drove me to the Southampton hospital, where I was born, to get it fixed up. Then he took me home and stood, embarrassed as a little boy, while my mother scolded him for letting me pick up the shot in the first place.

On weekends during the summer I stayed at Grandpa Skonieczny's and slept in the same bed with Uncle Mike, who is twelve years older than I am. When Uncle Mike was courting Theresa Hodukavich, whom he later married, he came in every Saturday at two or three in the morning. My grandfather didn't object, as long as Uncle Mike got up to do the chores. At six o'clock Grandpa Skonieczny would stand at the foot of the stairs, yelling, "Mike, get up." I always woke up, but Uncle Mike never moved. There was no sense in my going back to sleep right away, because I knew that Grandpa Skonieczny would yell again in five minutes, since Uncle Mike wouldn't move. Sure enough, when the five minutes were up, Grandpa Skonieczny would bawl, "Mike!" and start up the stairs. Then Uncle Mike would jump out of bed, get dressed, and run, and all would be quiet again.

Uncle Mike was the youngest of all the Skoniecznys and Yastrzemskis of his generation, and I was the oldest of mine. He married Aunt Theresa in the first family wedding I remember attending, and although I was only twelve years old I saw it through from beginning to end. Polish weddings traditionally last several days, but this one went only about twelve hours. It began at two in the afternoon and ended around two in the morning, and I made it all the way. I remember most of the details, including vivid impressions of Aunt Theresa's red hair beneath her bridal veil, the buckets of food we all ate, the endless polkas everybody danced, and the marvelous sliding races the kids had on the slippery sawdust floor.

The wedding was on November 25, 1951, at Saint Isadore's Church in Riverhead, twenty miles west of Bridgehampton. I have no idea how many people were there, but there must have been at least two hundred—about a hundred each from Mike's side of the family and Theresa's. Father Steve of Saint Isadore's— Polish Catholics nearly always refer to their priests by first names instead of last—performed the ceremony. Walter Jasinski, a cousin of Mike's, was the best man, and Mary Kazel, Theresa's closest friend, the maid of honor. After the ceremony the wedding party went to have pictures taken, and after that the festivities began.

Theresa's family had hired the Rainbow Room, a Polish club in Riverhead, where we started with a huge roast-beef dinner. The tables were family-style, long and narrow, with square openings here and there so people could go out to the dance floor. There was a band—all brasses, if I remember correctly—which had come from somewhere down the island, and, believe me, I've never seen a band work as hard as those guys did. At a Polish wedding every dance is a polka, and the music is practically continuous. That night it went on hour after hour, with cousins and aunts and uncles and great-aunts and great-uncles and nephews and nieces dancing and dancing to—and maybe beyond—exhaustion.

Everybody but me danced all night. I'm probably the only

Pole in the whole world who can't dance the polka. My mother spent years trying to teach me, but every minute was wasted. At Uncle Mike's and Aunt Theresa's wedding, she kept coming back to drag me out on the floor, and so did all the rest of my female relatives and also Aunt Theresa and all of hers. I went out and skipped around a little, but that was all. I didn't know how to dance the polka, didn't want to learn, never would learn, and never will. As a matter of fact, not only the polka but every other kind of dance throws me.

While grownups were ducking around us to get out to the floor, the other kids and I raced each other on the sawdust. It was a big hall, and you could slide from one end of it to the other without stopping. We had speed races and endurance races and relay races and every other kind of race you can think of, and the polkas blared in our ears and people danced all around us. That band played on and on, and everyone danced on and on. I remember being absolutely amazed at the endurance of those people, especially the women. The polka is a fast dance, and there's rarely a break in it, but none of them seemed to get tired. Even the band went steadily for something like four hours before resting. By then, it was time to eat again.

At the Rainbow Room they had dart games and shuffleboard, both of which I was pretty good at. Since none of my cousins was old enough to play these games with me, I got my uncles off the dance floor every so often. I guess they were just as happy to get away from those polkas for a while. I don't think they could keep up with the women.

The bride and groom left about an hour before midnight, but that didn't hold up the party or stop the band from playing polkas or keep me from going back and forth between the sawdust surface and the playroom. Bushed as I was, I played darts and shuffleboard and slid along the floor until my eyes drooped and my head nodded, but I wouldn't leave before the last gun was fired. By then the younger kids had long since gone to bed, but I represented their generation right to the end. The boys in the band were sleepily putting away their instruments when my parents bundled me into the car for the drive back to Bridge-hampton.

From the time I was small I can remember everyone in the family talking about potato prices. We knew by the end of August whether the year would be good or bad. If Dad came home and said, "They're going for two dollars," it meant we'd get along all right; or if he said, "Two and a quarter," it meant maybe a new car. But if he said, "They're going for a dollar and a quarter," it meant we were in for a rough year. The break-even point was $1.75 a hundredweight. Anything under that was bad news; anything over, good. The most prosperous times I remember were the Korean War years, when we got three new cars in a row. Then the market sagged, and we drove the same car for four years.

My dad and his brother Tommy are partners, as they have been since they inherited a potato farm in Bridgehampton from their uncle Vincent Zaluski. It was during the busy seasons, especially at harvest time in late summer and early fall, that all the grown-ups in the family, including my mother, worked hardest. I was too small to do much until the summer after my freshman year at Bridgehampton High School, when I had a variety of jobs: moving irrigation pipes, tying cauliflower, cutting cabbage, picking cucumbers, and helping to load trucks.

I liked loading trucks best because, although tough, it was the most fun. Since we didn't have the sophisticated equipment the family owns now, we did everything the hard way. The potatoes had to be picked by hand and put into bags weighing seventy-five or eighty pounds, which then were stacked about eight high on the backs of trucks. While a truck moved slowly between two rows of potato bags, two men lifted the bags onto the truck and two others, riding in the truck, piled the bags up on one of the stacks. This was the part I enjoyed, because the stacks were usually wobbly and it was quite a trick to put a heavy bag on top of a stack without the whole thing collapsing.

My dad, who insisted I do only the type of work that would

strengthen my wrists and arms for baseball, and nothing that might cause an injury, didn't want me hoisting bags up from the ground, but he let me work in the trucks, which gave me all the exercise I needed, and I still had the fun of stacking bags.

I was too busy in high school to see as much of Grandpa Skonieczny as I wanted to, which bothered me, because his physical condition was steadily deteriorating. He came to ball games when he could, and when he couldn't I went to tell him about them as soon as possible after they were over. We continued to go to Sag Harbor for the Saturday-night movies until the summer of 1957, right after I graduated from high school and just before I entered Notre Dame. By then he was too sick to leave the house. His case of Parkinson's disease had become so advanced that only a brain operation could stop his terrible shaking. When I left for college that September, he had already decided to have it.

"I'm scared, Grandpa," I said. "It's a risky operation."

"I can't go on like this," he said.

"Well, I don't want you to die."

"Don't worry, sonny, I won't die," he said. "The next time you see me I'll be as healthy as you."

We said good-by and I went to South Bend. The first member of the faculty I met there, the prefect of religion, became one of my closest friends. A young priest named Father Glenn Boarman, he was a suave, handsome man of medium height, with black hair and dark brown eyes, and he had a variety of interests, not the least of which was baseball. He knew I was at Notre Dame on a baseball scholarship, and he greeted me with the warmth of an old friend. We hit it off on sight, and soon I was going to him with all my problems.

The one that gnawed most was the operation facing Grandpa Skonieczny. Over and over I told Father Boarman, "I'm afraid I'll never see him again." And over and over he said, "I'm sure he'll be all right. All you can do is pray."

And that was all I did on the day of the operation, when Father Boarman gave me permission to cut classes. I divided my time between the chapel at Breen Phillips Hall, where I lived, on the east end of the campus, and the grotto beside the Rockne Memorial on the far northwest end. Nearly every Notre Dame student makes a daily pilgrimage to the grotto. An exact replica of the Lady of Lourdes shrine in France, it consists of a cave built into the side of a hill, with a statue of the Blessed Virgin on the plateau, and a stream that never runs dry. You light a candle inside the cave, then come out and pray on one of the three thousand kneeling-benches in front of the Virgin.

I usually went there in the evenings with my buddies Ron Zak and Bernie Dobransky. On the day of Grandpa Skonieczny's operation I prayed there alone, and later in the day, when they were free, Ron and Bernie joined me. I moved back and forth between there and the chapel perhaps three times during the day. Just before supper, I had a phone call from my mother.

"He's all right," she said. "He's all right. Isn't that wonderful!"

All I could say was, "Thank God," and soon both Mom and I were laughing and crying and interrupting each other as we babbled back and forth.

The next day she called again.

"We saw him at the hospital," she said. "He isn't shaking, and he looks fine. He's very anxious to see the place where you're going to school."

"You mean he's coming out here?" I said.

"Dad and I will drive out to get you for Christmas vacation," she said. "Grandma and Grandpa are coming along."

"Is it all right?" I asked. "Are you sure it's all right?"

"The doctor says he'll be able to travel then, that the trip will do him good," Mom said.

"When can he go home from the hospital?"

"Friday," she said.

For the next four days I spent nearly as much time in the grotto and the chapel as at classes. I counted the hours to Friday and the days to Christmas vacation, which was three weeks away. When I saw Father Boarman, all I could talk about was Grandpa

Skonieczny and the wonderful operation which had made him well.

"When he gets here," I said, "you're the first person I want him to meet."

My mother called Friday morning to tell me they were going to pick up Grandpa Skonieczny at the hospital that afternoon. "He's feeling better every day," she said. "He can't wait to talk to you."

"And I can't wait to talk to him," I said.

I whistled and laughed my way through the day, stopping in at the chapel from time to time to say prayers of thanks. *In three weeks, I kept thinking, he'll be here. I can see him in three weeks. I can show him the campus and the buildings and the ball field and the chapel where I prayed for him. I can introduce him to Father Boarman and to all the wonderful guys I've met. In three weeks—three weeks . . .*

Next summer, I kept thinking, we can go fishing together. I'll find time between ball games—I'll make time. I'll get over to see him every day, if it's just for a minute. And he can go wherever I go, to see me play ball. And on Saturday nights he and Grandma and I can see the early show at Sag Harbor.

It'll be crabbing season before I come back to college, I kept thinking. We'll get some chicken heads and some line and go to the inlet and get ourselves a bushel of crabs and take them home for Grandma to boil and the whole family, Grandpa Skonieczny and all, will eat them. . . .

Back at the dormitory to get ready for supper, I took the stairs three at a time, humming and laughing to myself like crazy. As I waved to guys I wanted to yell, "Grandpa Skonieczny's home now! And he's coming out here in less than three weeks!" And as I combed my hair I looked at myself in the mirror and grinned, and there seemed to be two of us happily waiting for Grandpa Skonieczny.

When I turned to leave, a guy I knew casually was standing at my door. "Father Boarman wants to see you in his office," he said.

"Father Boarman?"

"Yes."

"What does he want?" I said.

"I don't know."

My heart jumped, but I thought, *It can't be anything very important. He's got something to show me. Or maybe he's trying to bring me back to earth so I'll pay more attention to my studies. It isn't anything—it can't be—*

Except that Father Boarman had never sent for me at that hour before.

His office was on the main floor of Breen Phillips Hall, four flights down from my room. I went to the window and looked out at a lone priest pacing back and forth in the crisp late November night, then took a long breath and left the room. Slowly, as though in a dream, I moved to the stairs and started down them, holding the banister rail, which felt smooth and clean.

When I reached the main floor my heart pounded and my stomach fluttered and my hands were clammy and I had to make myself move along the corridor. As I approached the door to Father Boarman's office I stopped, clenched my fists, closed my eyes, and heaved a deep sigh. I took one step, then a few more, then paused in front of the door before knocking.

"Come in."

Now I was inside, looking into Father Boarman's dark eyes. "Sit down," he said gently. Then: "Carl, I have bad news."

"Grandpa Skonieczny?"

"Pray for his soul, Carl," Father Boarman said. "He died this afternoon."

CHAPTER 3

Family Ball Club

I'm told that when I was eighteen months old my dad got me a tiny baseball bat, which I dragged around wherever I went, the way other babies drag blankets or favorite toys. I vaguely remember playing catch with him as a very small boy, but my first clear memory is hitting tennis balls in the back yard against his pitching after supper every night when I was about six. Later we played make-believe ball games between the Yankees and the Red Sox, my two favorite teams, going through the line-ups with me batting left-handed or right, whichever way the real ballplayers batted. Dad would decide each time I connected if it was a hit or an out, and after three outs we switched to the other team. But whichever team was up, I did all the hitting and he did all the pitching.

When Rich was old enough, he took Dad's place in our Yankee–Red Sox games with tennis balls. He was usually the Yankees, and we changed off hitting and pitching, inning by inning. We had a rather elaborate set of rules. The plate was near the garage in back of our house, which we designated as left field, while Mr. Ruppel's house next door was right field. Anything that cleared the houses was a home run, with singles, doubles, and triples determined by where they landed. Most line drives were hits, but fly balls were outs if they hit any part of either house. Ours was a shingle house, and Mr. Ruppel's was stucco. Although we knocked some of his stucco off, he was really pretty good about it. Once in a while, if we belted the house two or three times in a row, he yelled something out the window, but that didn't happen often. Most hitters were right-handed, and we were more apt to pull the ball and hit our own house in left field.

Bill McNamara, who lived a couple of doors down the street and played for the Bridgehampton Blue Sox, liked to come over and pitch tennis balls to me when I was the batting star of our Little League team. I took a broken bat and cut it down almost to the trade mark, and Bill, who stood about six feet four and could throw real hard, tried to get the ball by me from forty feet away. When he couldn't, he moved closer and closer, but even at twenty-five feet he seldom succeeded in keeping me from getting a piece of the ball. It was great for my wrists, because I had to get that little bat around tremendously fast, and it helped sharpen my vision because I couldn't take my eye off the ball for a split second.

When I was old enough to use a regular baseball instead of a tennis ball, Dad and I played our old Yankee–Red Sox games on the fair grounds, a big lot across the street from our house. Using the side of a building for a backstop, I hit for an hour or more after supper with Dad pitching to me. He threw nothing but fast balls, taking a dozen balls, throwing them until they were gone, then shagging them while I stood at the plate practicing my swing. Rich helped shag when he was big enough, and sometimes Bill McNamara gave us a hand.

On Grandpa Skonieczny's farm I gathered stones and peewee potatoes and anything else that was hittable, and played stickball behind his barn. I'd hit fungo-style until he got in from the fields, imagining each swing as a hit or an out as I played a make-believe ball game between the Red Sox and the Yankees. Even during the busy season I found time to hit stones or peewees. We

Family Ball Club

moved irrigation pipes in shifts, working three hours and resting two. I'd get so absorbed in a game during the rest period that I had to be called when it was time to go back to the irrigation pipes.

One of my best friends was Tony Tiska, a boy my age, whose father owned a 125-acre farm in Bridgehampton. Mr. Tiska was always looking for help. When we were old enough he paid us as much as $25 to move pipes on Saturdays when his regular people took off. Tony and I would quit at about two in the afternoon and play stickball in an enclosure where the balls ricocheted around and we didn't have to shag them. Instead of Red Sox–Yankee games, we played all-star games so we could pack the line-ups any way we wanted. I picked all left-handers and Tony all right-handers. My two favorites were Ted Williams and Joe Collins—Williams because he was Williams and Collins, then the Yankee first baseman, because he was Polish.

I was so eager to hit every day that I doped out a gadget, which Uncle Mike made for me, that allowed me to practice without shagging, even when I was alone. I put a ball on top of a few feet of movable rubber hose attached to the outside of a stationary iron pipe driven into the ground. Uncle Mike drilled holes in the hose and the pipe, so I could adjust the top of the hose at any level between my knees and my shoulders and secure it to the pipe with a screw through the corresponding holes. He also drilled a hole through the ball and inserted a wire, to which I tied about two hundred feet of string for reeling in the ball after I hit it. When there was nobody to play with, I took my contraption across to the fair grounds and worked with it for as long as I liked. It was a good way to learn the strike zone, because I had to adjust my swing to various levels as I moved the hose up and down.

I went through Little League and Babe Ruth baseball, playing various positions for various teams. Shortstop was my best spot, but I had a good arm and often pitched or caught. I was the catcher for the Bridgehampton Lions Little League team, and I played short and pitched for the South Fork Little Leaguers.

South Fork reached the finals of the state championships before Ossining eliminated us, which was hardly a disgrace. In our area we had fewer kids to draw from than most, and what we lacked in quantity we made up for in quality.

In the Babe Ruth League I once pitched a no-hitter, but I played short most of the time because Dad, who coached the team, wanted me to get as much experience as possible at the position he thought I'd always be playing. We had a great club, winning the state title and attracting attention from baseball scouts, who, although they couldn't touch us because we were too young, followed us pretty closely during the summer.

I did well playing with boys my own age, but I had trouble competing with older kids when I made the high-school varsity as a 120-pound thirteen-year-old freshman shortstop. I had never played on anything bigger than Little League diamonds, which are considerably smaller than fields of regulation dimensions. Besides, I was the smallest and youngest boy in the high-school league, and, lacking the strength to hit the ball hard against the pitching of boys sixteen and seventeen, I had to bunt my way on base. I used to push the ball down the third-base line and beat throws to first. Even though I piled up a good batting average that way, I knew a hitter can't live on bunts alone and was very unhappy about it.

"I don't want to be a bunter, Dad," I said. "What can I do?"

"Well," he said, "you'll be bigger next year, and I'm sure you'll do much better. Your wrist action is good and you're a natural hitter. I think if you work this winter with a lead bat it will develop your arm and shoulder muscles, but it won't be much fun."

It wasn't, especially in freezing weather with an east wind often roaring in from the ocean. I kept the bat in the garage and made the frigid one-hundred-foot trip there from the house in a huge old sheepskin coat too bulky to wear for anything else. About an hour before supper every night I put on the coat, ran out of the house and into the garage, grabbed the lead bat, and started swinging it the minute I got my fingers on it. It usually took me ten or fifteen minutes to warm up enough to discard the coat, and I spent the rest of the time swinging the bat and doing calisthenics with it. Then I put the big coat on and rushed back to the house.

It all paid off in the spring. Thanks to the combination of long hours with the lead bat and my natural growth, I was much bigger and stronger than I had been the year before, and now I could compete with any kids of high-school age. I really had an amazing season, especially at the plate. I ended up with a .650 batting average and at one point had a streak of 15 straight hits.

Because nobody else could catch, I took the job, although I hadn't liked it in the Babe Ruth League. Scared to death I'd break a finger, I exposed only my glove hand, keeping the other one behind my back when the ball was pitched and letting the ball hit my chest protector or shin guards if I missed it. Although I must have looked awkward, I impressed some of the scouts who came out to our games, partly because I had a good arm and wasn't afraid to use it to throw to any base, but mostly because of the way I handled Billy DePetris, our star pitcher.

DePetris, a short heavy-set boy with black wavy hair and dark eyes, was a senior, three or four years older than I, with one of the biggest-breaking knuckle curve balls I ever saw. When he got it over the plate he was tough to hit, but when he didn't he was wild low. Although the ball would hit the dirt in front of me, I always managed to scoop it up one-handed, and nothing impresses a scout more than a young catcher who can handle pitches that skid along the ground. The scouts who watched me were the same guys who had seen me in Babe Ruth baseball. They still couldn't talk to my folks or me because I was too young, but there was no law against their looking. I learned later that Long Island scouts from all over the major leagues came to see me hit and catch. But catching was not for me. That was the only year I ever tried it in high school.

While baseball was my first love, I played basketball all through high school and would have played football if Dad hadn't stopped me for fear I might get hurt. I quarterbacked our six-man team as a junior, then gave up the game without regrets. Basketball was something else again. I had always liked to fool around under a hoop hung over our garage door, and, since I knew I'd never be tall enough to compete with big men around the basket, I practiced long shots for years. Eventually I developed an accurate one-handed peg shot, a sort of line drive, much like the one which Tommy Heinsohn used when he played for the Boston Celtics. It was good enough to give me the schoolboy scoring championship of Suffolk County my last two years. As a senior I averaged 34 points a game, which I think still stands as a Suffolk County schoolboy record. Nearly all my baskets were from 30 feet out or more.

But I never had serious basketball ambitions. I was first and foremost a baseball player, and all my hopes for the future rested in baseball. For a time I had ambitions to be a switch-hitter like Mickey Mantle, but Dad put the clamp on that. I could hit for distance right-handed, but I missed the ball too often because I couldn't see it as well from that side of the plate. As a switch-hitter I might have improved my home-run production by batting right-handed against left-handed pitching, but I would have struck out more often. Left-handers didn't bother me that much anyhow.

Dad's decision for me to concentrate on being a left-handed hitter was undoubtedly the right one. He was an excellent judge of talent and how it should be handled. If I am a great ballplayer, he made me one. I had the instincts and the drive and the latent ability, but he brought them all out and helped me take full advantage of them. He talked baseball by the hour, discussing fine points in detail, inventing situations and explaining how to cope with them, doing all the things with me that any good coach does with a promising young prospect.

For years Dad was the star shortstop of the Riverhead Falcons, one of the best semi-pro teams in the East. They played most of the other outstanding semi-pro clubs, including such famous outfits as the House of David, the Bushwicks, and the Homestead

Grays. The Falcons played Tuesdays and Thursdays, and when they were home I was their batboy. I formed a mutual admiration society with Carl Braun, their best pitcher, who was one of the top stars of the National Basketball Association. He liked me, and I hero-worshiped him as a big national name in one of my favorite sports and a big local name in the other.

Short, sturdy, and tremendously powerful, Dad piled up fantastic batting averages (often over .500 for a summer season) and could also hit for distance. If he had started early enough, he might have made it to the big leagues, despite a peculiar throwing style which looked awkward even though it was effective. He could make all the plays and throw with speed and accuracy, and he did the right things at the right time.

He was a semi-pro only because he didn't have the time, the money, or the chance to be anything else. At twenty-three, after I was born, he tried out with the Cardinals and the Dodgers, but he was too old and too tied down with responsibilities to start at the bottom of organized baseball's ladder. The Cardinal tryout was at a rookie school in Morristown, New Jersey, but nothing came of it. Later that same summer he went with a friend to Ebbets Field in Brooklyn for the Dodger tryout. The best they offered was a Class D contract, which he couldn't afford to accept. I think that was the end of his hopes, the time when he truly transferred his big-league ambitions to me.

Oddly enough, with all his concentration on baseball, he insisted—in fact, demanded—that I acquire a college education. Never having gone beyond the eighth grade himself, he knew the handicaps of inadequate education and he wanted Rich and me to avoid them. He even saw baseball advantages in college for me. "If you go to a place where there's a good baseball program," he once said, "you'll be playing the equivalent of Class B ball and getting an education at the same time." Whenever we talked of my future in baseball, it was always with the understanding that I would go to college first, or, if necessary, while I was playing professionally.

Before I was born Dad had formed the Bridgehampton White

Eagles, a most remarkable team, for it was originally made up almost exclusively of members of our family. Dad was the manager and shortstop, and the rest of the team included Tommy, Chet, Ray, and Stan, his four brothers; Mike and Jerry Skonieczny, my mother's brothers; Walter and Leo Jasinski, their cousins; and Alex Borkowski, another cousin. As time went on, outsiders came in to fill gaps left by retiring players, but for years the backbone of the White Eagles was the Yastrzemski and Skonieczny clans. Chet and Tommy, who was the first to quit because of a bad leg injury, were pitchers; Stan was a catcher; Ray and Dad were infielders, the Skonieczny brothers outfielders, Walter Jasinski a first baseman, his brother Leo an outfielder, and Alex Borkowski a second baseman.

The White Eagles played Sundays, and everyone in the family, Yastrzemskis, Skoniecznys, Jasinskis, and Borkowskis, went out to cheer them on. Grandpa Skonieczny and Grandpa Yastrzemski always went together—one drove the other—and, since I spent Saturday nights at Grandpa Skonieczny's, I went with them. I became the White Eagles' batboy when I was seven. Dad dug up an ancient first baseman's glove that was bigger than my head, and I shagged flies for the White Eagles with it. The glove had a big thumb attached to the rest of its hand with webbing that was always breaking and which I always had to restring. Old and beat-up as it was, I loved that glove and kept it around for years.

There were so many semi-pro teams around that the Eastern Suffolk County League was divided into North and South Shore divisions. We had two teams in Bridgehampton, the White Eagles and the Blue Sox, both in the South Shore division, along with teams in towns like Southampton, Easthampton, Montauk, Amagansett, and Hampton Bays. The biggest towns in the North Shore division were Riverhead and Mattituck. The season began in early June and ended in mid-September because most of the teams used college boys who had to get back to school. The division winners played each other for the league championship, which the White Eagles often won.

Dad was their founder, manager, general manager, treasurer, traveling secretary—everything. If it hadn't been for him, they probably would have folded before my time, but he kept them alive long enough for me to play three years with them. I must have been one of the youngest semi-pro ballplayers of all time because I started in 1954 at fourteen; I turned fifteen that August. By then the Blue Sox were long gone, several of the other teams in the league were faltering, and the White Eagles themselves needed new blood. Most of my uncles were nearing or over forty, sick of baseball, and more inclined toward the beach than the diamond. They continued to play only at Dad's insistence.

The line-up, with variations depending on who showed up or felt like playing, was fairly well set. Uncle Chet, despite an arm that was beginning to give him the miseries, still did most of our pitching. Uncle Stosh (Stan) and Albie Musnicki, who, although not related to the family had been with the team for years, were the catchers, but both were ready to call it a career. With Walter Jasinski in irrevocable retirement, our first baseman was Bill Stravopoulos, a big, handsome, black-haired Greek boy who was another of my close friends and played on the high-school team with me. The rest of the infield and all the outfield were family—Alex Borkowski at second, Dad at short, Uncle Ray (with some reluctance, because he wanted to quit too) at third, Uncle Jerry or Leo Jasinski in left, me in center, and Uncle Mike in right.

That was my only year in the outfield, but there was no choice, for the only way Dad could get the others to play was to let them stay in positions they knew. Although I've been an outfielder throughout my big-league career, I didn't like playing there for the White Eagles. We often performed on fields without fences, which meant playing good hitters about a mile out, because anything that went past the outfielders was a sure home run. On the other hand, hits that would be home runs in any big-league ball park were almost automatic outs because we played so deep. Routine fly balls went for singles or doubles because we were too far out to catch them. And we had to do so much running that our tongues were hanging out if many balls were hit to the outfield. It was a dog's life, and after one season I was glad to get back to the infield, where I felt I belonged.

Although close to forty, Dad was the guts of the ball club, a good shortstop and the best hitter on the team. He was sort of a right-handed Ted Williams, for, being a pull hitter, he faced packed defenses to left field, just as Williams faced packed defenses to right. In Dad's case the third baseman played almost on the foul line and back on the grass; the shortstop was also deep and well to his right, the second baseman on the third-base side of second, the left fielder near the foul line, the center fielder in left, and the right fielder in center. The only one guarding the right side of the diamond was the first baseman, who had to play close enough to the bag to cover it in case of an infield grounder. Dad could have broken up the shift by placing the ball to right field once in a while, but, like Williams, who wouldn't hit to the opposite field either, he was too proud and too stubborn. Batting right into the shift, he was still a consistent .450 hitter who also collected his share of home runs.

He always batted in the cleanup spot, with me third, right ahead of him. If we were the first two men up in an inning, the two of us went as close to the plate as the umpire would let us while the opposing pitcher was warming up; then Dad would discuss with me what we should look for. But the thing I remember best about him was that he almost never struck out—maybe once a year. And I never saw him strike out swinging, only when the umpire called him out, a circumstance that drove him crazy. I never saw anyone get madder at the umpire after being called out on strikes than Dad. It was not only a terrible blow to his pride but an insult to his baseball intelligence, because he figured he knew more about the strike zone than the umpire did.

Stan Michna, a good friend and bowling partner of Dad's who umpired most of our home games, once called him out for the third out of the inning in a game with the Montauk Army base team, and Dad was so mad I thought he'd have a stroke. First he whirled around and screamed, *"What?"*

"Strike three," Michna yelled, "you're out!"

Dad dropped his bat, pointed to the ground, and yelled, "It was down at my ankles."

"It was right over the plate," Michna yelled.

The two of them stood nose to nose for about a minute, hollering at each other. Finally, as we all knew he would, Michna pulled out a stopwatch and said, "You have thirty seconds to get out to your position."

"Come on, Dad," I said, "he's not going to change."

"Well, I'm not going out there," Dad said.

"Twenty-seven, twenty-six, twenty-five . . ." Michna intoned.

Dad marched to the bench and sat down, and the rest of us gathered around him, pleading with him to take the field. He folded his arms, glared at Michna, and refused to move.

"Nineteen, eighteen, seventeen . . ." Michna said.

"The ball was low," Dad said.

"Sixteen, fifteen, fourteen . . ."

"Hey, Carl," somebody said, "if he throws you out, we'll forfeit the game. We've only got nine guys."

"I don't care," Dad said. "It wasn't a strike."

Mom poked her head out of our car, parked near the foul line, and yelled, "Come on, come on, get out of there."

"Nine, eight, seven . . ."

"You want the game to be forfeited, Dad?" I said. "It's only a strikeout."

"It wasn't a strikeout," Dad said. Then, taking his eyes off Michna for the first time, he glared at me and said, *"I don't strike out."*

"Six, five, four . . ."

"Come on, come on—"

"Three, two . . ."

Dad stood up, gave Michna one last withering look, picked up his glove, and started for his position. Everyone, including the rest of the guys on the team, broke into a cheer, we all headed for the field, and the crisis was over.

Even Dad's enthusiasm and insistence couldn't turn back the clock the next year, when more members of the family balked at giving their Sundays to the White Eagles. After all, the Hamptons are a big resort area that attracts vacationers all the way from New York, and here my uncles were living practically on the water and wasting their one precious day off from a tough week's work playing a young man's game on sandlot ball fields.

They were older, achier, creakier, and sicker than ever of a Sunday routine that was becoming as tough for them as any weekday in the potato fields. On the alternate Sundays when we played on the road it wasn't so bad, because we had the morning off and seldom went more than half an hour's drive from Bridgehampton. But when we played at home it was murder, because, as nobody took care of the high-school field during the week, we had to fix it up ourselves for the Sunday game.

Dad and I got up early, went around in the pickup truck for a few Skoniecznys and Yastrzemskis, and made eight-o'clock Mass at the Queen of the Most Holy Rosary Church on the Montauk Highway. If Father Joe didn't give a long sermon we were out by eight-thirty and off for the ball field behind the school a mile or so up the road. Since Father Joe was a baseball fan and never missed a game, he was pretty good about keeping his sermons short on the Sundays we played at home. After Mass we raked the infield diamond by hand, then tied a mat to the back of the pickup truck and ran it back and forth over the dirt until it was smoothed down. Finally we limed the field, marking out the batters' and coaches' boxes, the foul lines, and the on-deck circles. All this took anywhere from two to two and a half hours. We hurried home for lunch, gulped down our food, put on our uniforms, and got back to the ball field in time for twelve-o'clock batting practice and a two-o'clock game.

My second year I moved to shortstop and Dad to third, and we picked up a couple more guys from my high-school team to fill in some of the gaps. Tony Tiska, by then a blond stocky boy an inch short of six feet, took my place in the outfield, and Billy De-

Petris came in to help out with the pitching. I did some pitching myself that year, but spent most of my time in the infield. When Alex Borkowski wasn't available, Dad played second, giving us a double-play combination of Yastrzemski, Yastrzemski, and Stravopoulos, a tongue-twister that tickled a lot of people, including John Murphy, then the Red Sox farm director. So did the fact that we were a father-son, not a brother, combination.

One day Murphy called Frank (Bots) Nekola, the Red Sox scout who had been following me for several years.

"How's Yastrzemski doing?" Murphy said.

"Great," Nekola said. "He's hitting .460, and his old man's hitting .480."

"Hey, Bots," said Murphy, "are you sure you're watching the right Yastrzemski?"

Dad hit some tremendous shots that went for home runs on ball fields that weren't wide open, but nothing gave him a bigger kick than the day he and I hit back-to-back homers in a game at Riverhead. This was one of the few ball parks in the league that had a fence around it. I came up in the fifth inning and belted a 380-foot drive that cleared the one in right center field. Then Dad followed with a smash that must have gone 450 feet over the left-field fence. We got five runs that inning but still lost the game, 12–10.

I hit more and more homers as the summer progressed, because there was a big potato lot in right field at Bridgehampton. Anything over 360 feet landed in the middle of it, and by late July the plants were so thick it was hard to find the ball. I pulled the ball as often as I could, because it was 500 feet to center, and a sock in that direction was just a long out. I never hit a home run to left, the wrong field for me, because the schoolhouse behind it was 400 feet from the plate. Dad hit the roof every so often, and I'm pretty sure was the only guy who ever cleared it.

The whole league, White Eagles and all, died after the summer of 1956. That was the worst year we had trying to get guys out to play. Dad and I went all over town Sunday mornings, begging uncles, cousins, friends, everybody to show up for ball games. Sometimes we did all the raking and smoothing and liming ourselves, although usually we could get Tony or Strav or Billy DePetris to help. We didn't consider that a problem at all. The big thing was to talk guys into playing before they headed for the beach. Once they did that, they were gone, because even if we could find them we'd never get them to leave. We always managed a full team, but only after a lot of running around and telephoning. And there wasn't a game that summer that somebody didn't play under protest.

My last two summers at home, when I was seventeen and eighteen, we had to go all the way to Lake Ronkonkoma, sixty miles down the island, to find a ball game. The Lake Ronkonkoma Cardinals were a good, fast semi-pro team that played night games Tuesdays and Thursdays and afternoon games Sundays. They paid Dad and me twenty bucks a game each and expenses. We didn't mind the Sunday games, but the night games were pretty tough. We finished on the farm at five in the afternoon; then Mom, Dad, Rich, and I jumped into the car and drove for an hour and fifteen minutes so we could get there in time for batting practice before an eight-o'clock game. After it ended— around eleven or eleven-thirty—we went to a restaurant for something to eat. Then Dad drove home while Rich and I slept in the back seat.

Our last year with the Cardinals was 1958, with Dad, then forty-one, playing third base and me shortstop. We still hit third and fourth in the batting order and he still murdered the ball, but by then he was creaking at the seams and the game was becoming an ordeal even for him. He never complained, but I could tell the only reason he played was on account of me, just as that had been the only reason he kept the White Eagles alive so long. But, forty-one or no forty-one, he was still an amazing hitter. That last year at Lake Ronkonkoma he outhit me by about 35 points. I finished somewhere around .375 and he hit about .410.

Just before I went back to Notre Dame for my sophomore year, we all drove down to Lake Ronkonkoma for a Sunday-afternoon game against Port Jefferson. Dad was up four times, flied out, doubled, grounded out, and singled—two for four, and, as usual, no strikeouts. Two months later I signed a contract with the Red Sox. From that day to this, my dad has never played another ball game.

CHAPTER 4

Bonus Fever

While I was growing up, my baseball heroes were Ted Williams and Stan Musial, but the guy I really envied was a pitcher named Paul Pettit, who, in a big-league career that lasted only two years, won one game and lost two for the Pittsburgh Pirates. Pettit was baseball's first $100,000 bonus player, and, when scouts came around to watch us play, that magic figure was on my mind. I thought about it when I went to bed at night, sometimes I dreamed about it, and I often talked about it. Yet in my own mind it seemed a pretty wild idea. One hundred thousand dollars is a lot of money, and after the unhappy Pettit experience I figured big-league ball clubs wouldn't be in a hurry to hand that much out to other untried schoolboys. Anyhow, as a seventeen-year-old senior at Bridgehampton High in the spring of 1957, I would have signed for any amount I was offered if it had been up to me.

But it wasn't up to me. As a minor, I couldn't sign anything. Dad was the boss, and behind him was Father Joe. For Father Joe—his last name was Ratkowski—was more than just a baseball fan. An outstanding athlete in his youth, he could have been a professional ballplayer if he hadn't chosen the priesthood. Before going to Bridgehampton he had had a parish in Brooklyn, where, like everyone else there, he was an ardent Dodger fan. He knew several big-league ballplayers well, and two, Erv Palica and later Don McMahon, had once been altar boys for him at Saint Jerome's Church. He also knew Gil Hodges, an old Brooklyn idol who now manages the Mets. Father Joe knew baseball and how to dicker for a baseball contract. Right from the time scouts began seriously talking to my folks about my future, Father Joe had told Dad, "Don't sign for less than six figures. He's worth it and you can get it." Dad had no intention of settling for less.

Father Joe hadn't inspired Dad's determination that I go to college, but he heartily approved. I don't know whether or not he was a Notre Dame man, but that was where he wanted me to go, and my parents agreed. They insisted on a Catholic college and considered Notre Dame the best. Furthermore, Dad had been listening to Notre Dame football games and watching them on television for years and had heard so much about the place he would have wanted me to go there even if I weren't an athlete. The clincher, if one were needed, was that Notre Dame had a good ball club, and Father Joe thought he could get me a baseball scholarship. So even before I graduated from high school in June of 1957, my parents had decided not to accept any big-league baseball offers at that time unless somebody came up with those magic six figures Father Joe had been talking about. Nor would my family consider college scholarship offers from anywhere except Notre Dame as long as there was a chance of my getting one there.

We received some pretty lush offers. Most of the metropolitan New York colleges were willing to give me full scholarships. So were Duke and Miami, both of which went very big for baseball. And a few other colleges came up with some fantastic packages that included, besides the conventional board, room, tuition, books, and laundry, spending money up to a hundred dollars a month, a complete new wardrobe, an apartment of my own, and a car. I had never owned even a jalopy, never had more than one suit, never slept in a room by myself, and, although Dad let me keep what I earned in the fields, had never had anywhere near a hundred dollars a month to spend.

Not being as fussy about Notre Dame as Mom and Dad, I wanted to grab one of those fancy scholarships. "What difference will it make if I don't go to Notre Dame?" I asked Dad. "A college education is a college education. Why can't I go to the place that offers the most?"

"Because Notre Dame is the best Catholic college in the country and that's where you're going," he said.

"I don't even see why I have to go to a Catholic college."

"Well, I do," he said. "So does your mother. And if Father Joe can arrange it, it will be Notre Dame."

In the meantime, as I continued to have a remarkable senior season, big-league scouts were more and more in evidence. My dad knew them all, but I couldn't keep track of them. There were sixteen clubs then, and most were represented at practically every game we played. We didn't have a regular pitcher that year. Tony Tiska, a fine outfielder and a consistent .400 hitter who could have signed with the Braves for a good bonus if he had wanted to go into baseball, did some of the pitching, and I did the rest. Tony could throw hard, but without false modesty I must admit I threw harder. I had an overhand fast ball that really dipped and moved around, a pretty good curve, and a change which I could use if the occasion demanded.

Perhaps most important of all for a kid my age, I had good control and could get the ball over the plate with something on it. But, although I liked to pitch and attracted some attention among scouts as a pitcher, hitting was my life. I got my biggest kicks out of belting the ball out of the park. And, thanks to that lead bat in the garage and all the other work I did, I had the strength to do it. By my senior year in high school I was nearly as strong as I am now.

Our last two games were for the Suffolk County schoolboy championship, the semi-finals against Bellport High and the finals against Center Moriches, both seven-inning games. Each school had over two thousand students, practically matching the entire population of Bridgehampton, and we shouldn't have been on the same field with either. Bellport had an especially good team that played clubs like Seton Hall and LaSalle Military Academy, prep schools with kids who averaged a year or two more than high-school boys in age.

I pitched against Bellport and, with scouts, farm directors, and other baseball officials in the stands, had quite an afternoon, giving one hit, striking out nineteen, and hitting a home run to help us win and get into the finals. That was on a Monday. On Thursday, pitching against Center Moriches, I threw a no-hitter, fanned twenty out of twenty-one and hit another homer.

As I was leaving the field I heard somebody say, "He was even better today than Monday."

"Oh," one of the guys on our team replied, "he had an off day Monday."

Not long after that, in an all-star game between the best Long Island schoolboys and the best from metropolitan New York, I pitched three innings, struck out all nine men I faced, and moved back to shortstop when I had finished pitching. I also hit a tremendous home run, a belt that must have gone well over 400 feet to deep right. On the way home after the game I said, "Do you suppose we'll hear from any scouts?"

"We might," Dad said. "But we're not signing any contracts."

"What if somebody offers six figures?"

"If it's plus college tuiton we'll consider it."

"You mean we'll turn down six figures if they don't add college tuition?" I said.

"You're going to college, son," he said. "If the college won't pay your tuition through a baseball scholarship—which it won't if you're a professional—then the team that signs you will."

A few days later we had a phone call from Lee MacPhail, then farm director and now general manager of the Yankees. "We'd like to have you come to the stadium for a workout," he said. "Can you make it tomorrow?"

"Yeah, sure—sure—well, look, I'll have to ask my dad," I stammered.

I handed Dad the phone, and he calmly confirmed a date for the next day. After he hung up I said, "The Yankees! Imagine! They want me to work out."

"You'll work out," Dad said.

"Can I sign with them?"

"Let's see what they offer."

"Dad," I said, "I've always wanted the Yankees. And now—"

"I know, son," he said. "So have I—first for me, now for you. I'll go see Father Joe."

When he came back, I asked what Father Joe had said.

" 'Stick to the six figures,' " Dad said, " 'and college tuition.' "

"Do you think they'll go that high?"

"I don't know," he said.

"Dad," I said, "what if they offer six figures and don't pay tuition? Can't we take that out of the bonus—for the Yankees?"

"We'll see."

As we drove in from Bridgehampton the next morning, all I could think about or talk about was the Yankees—Mantle and Bauer and Berra and Skowron and Macdougald and Ford and Kubek and all the rest. "Imagine, Dad," I said, "I'm going to dress in the same locker room with those guys. Maybe I'll even meet them."

"I know," he said.

"Think of it! Meeting Mickey Mantle! Maybe even playing with him."

"I know."

"Dad," I said, "how long do you think it would take me to get up to the Yankees?"

"You haven't signed with them yet."

"Don't you think I will?"

"Depends," Dad said.

It was a little after eleven when we pulled up in front of the players' entrance at Yankee Stadium. Ray Garland, who scouted Long Island for the Yankees and had been following my career ever since my freshman year in high school, was waiting for us. As we got out of the car I paused for just a second, looking at the gate and imagining what was inside.

Some day—maybe soon—I'll be going through this very gate on my own, I thought. *And kids will look at me and say, "There's Carl Yastrzemski." And they'll ask me for my autograph and I'll stop and sign it. And everywhere I go people will be saying. "There's Yastrzemski, the Yankee shortstop." . . . "There's Yastrzemski, the batting champion." . . . "There's Yastrzemski, the home-run king." . . . "There's the latest of the great Yankees—Ruth, Gehrig, DiMaggio, Mantle, Yastrzemski. That's Yastrzemski." . . .*

". . . sit over by the Yankee dugout," Ray Garland was saying. "I'll join you. Come on, Carl."

He led me beneath the stands to the Yankee locker room, where he turned me over to an equipment man and said, "This is Carl Yastrzemski. Give him a uniform and a place to dress." As I followed the guy across the spacious Yankee locker room, I recognized Mantle, Ford, Skowron, Kubek, and Bauer standing near the trainer's room, and thought, *Boy, I'd love to meet them. I wonder if he'll introduce me.* But he led me right past them and into a small room hardly bigger than a closet. He pointed to a uniform in a locker and said, "That ought to fit. Put it on." Then he left.

Two kids were in the room, both getting into Yankee uniforms. I found out later they were batboys. Neither paid any attention to me or the other, dressing in almost sullen silence. I wished somebody would say something but was too shy to start a conversation myself. I took off my jacket, hung it up, then got ready to put on the uniform.

As I dressed, one of the players was saying, "I got a job offer from a bank in Kansas City—two hundred a week. I think I'll take it. You can live pretty well on two hundred a week in Kansas City."

"Two hundred a week?" somebody said. "That's peanuts."

"Not in Kansas City," the player said. "I can do all right. My

YAZ

home's all paid for and my kids are coming along. I'll think I'll
take the job."

"You ought to be able to do better than that," a guy said.
"Sure I ought to be able to do better," was the reply, "but
I won't. I could have, if I'd grabbed the chances I got when I was
going good. I passed everything up. Now it's too late."

"The Yankees haven't dumped you yet," somebody said.

"No, but they will," the first guy said. "I'm through. I know it.
And I'm not going to monkey around in the minors. I'll tell you
guys something. While you have it, take advantage of it. Don't let
these good opportunities go by, the way I did. I was crazy. Now I
have to settle for two bills a week in Kansas City."

I got into a pair of white pin-striped pants, then put on the
shirt with the monogram NY in blue letters on the front. Even
though there was no number on the back, it was a thrill to wear
what was then the most famous uniform in baseball. But as I but-
toned the shirt I suddenly felt terribly lonely. Here were those
ballplayers I wanted so badly to meet, within ten feet of me, and
I couldn't talk to them. Here was one of them, giving advice
to those younger guys, and I couldn't listen to him without feeling like an eavesdropper. Here were those unfriendly little batboys practically touching me but paying not the least attention
to me. As I adjusted the cap I wished I could shake hands with
just one Yankee ballplayer so when I got home to Bridgehampton I could tell the kids I had met him.

Ray Garland was at the locker-room door, and he led me
through the runway to the dugout. A slight man with dark eyes
and the number 2 on the back of his Yankee uniform was standing on the field at the top of the dugout steps. It was Frank
Crosetti, the veteran coach.

"He's going to hit, Crow," Ray said, then went up into the
stands to join Dad.

"Okay, kid," Crosetti said. "Follow me."

As he led the way to the cage, where the Yankee irregulars
were taking batting practice, I noticed a couple of guys on the
Cleveland Indians, who were playing the Yankees that day, toss-

· 58 ·

ing a ball back and forth in front of the third-base dugout. Behind them somebody was taking a picture of Larry Doby swinging a bat. I stood a moment and swung my own, while Crosetti said to nobody in particular, "This kid goes in next."

The Yankee in the cage took two or three more swings and stepped out, and I moved into his place. As I dug in at the plate and looked down at the batting-practice pitcher—I never did know who it was—I felt very comfortable, loose, and confident. The pitcher wound up and threw a fast ball right down the middle. I hit it on a line to center field. I missed the next pitch, fouled one off, then put two into the right-field seats. The pitcher indicated he'd throw a curve, and I hit that along the ground, but the next one went into the stands in right. After about ten swings, including a fourth smash into the right-field bleachers, Crosetti yelled, "Okay, that's enough."

I started to run down the first-base line, figuring they wanted me to work out in the field, but Crosetti yelled, "Go in!" so I turned toward the dugout. Garland met me at the top of the steps and said, "Go get dressed. Mr. MacPhail wants to see you."

"What about infield?" I said.

"Don't bother," Ray said. "Put on your clothes and I'll take you upstairs." I learned later that they rushed me away before the Indians could find out who I was.

I showered and dressed without exchanging a word with anyone; then Ray led me up to Lee MacPhail's office. Dad was already there, and as soon as Ray and I arrived we were taken right in. MacPhail, a slight, blond, young-looking man, shook hands with Dad and me, invited us to sit down, and said, "Carl, would you like to play for the Yankees?"

"I sure would," I said.

"We think you can make it," MacPhail said. "We'll send you out for a while, and you'll be up here before you know it."

He turned to Dad. "We'll give him forty thousand dollars to sign," he said.

With all the talking we had done about six-figure bonuses, this was the first time we had actually had an offer. None of us

YAZ

had ever seen $40,000 in our lives, and I couldn't believe Dad would turn it down, but he did.

"It's not enough, Mr. MacPhail," he said.

MacPhail's eyes widened. "It's more than the Yankees have ever offered a high-school boy before," he said.

"It still isn't enough," Dad said.

"Take it, Dad," I said. "It's the *Yankees*."

"Forty thousand dollars is a lot of money, Mr. Yastrzemski," MacPhail said.

I pleaded with Dad with my eyes, started to say something, then saw his look and shut up. MacPhail talked a bit about the Yankees and what it meant to play for them, and how I could win fame and make a fortune almost in my home town, and what a big thing it would be for me to play with Mantle and Berra and Kubek and Ford and all those guys, and Dad sat and listened. Then he said, "I'll have to think about it."

"Fine," MacPhail said. "You think about it. I'm sure you'll change your mind. How much time do you want?"

"Oh, a couple of days," Dad said. "Maybe Ray can come out to the house, and we'll see then."

Back in Bridgehampton, Dad said to Father Joe, "The Yankees offered forty thousand. Sonny wants it. What do you think?"

"Don't take it," Father Joe said. "It's not enough."

"Even the Yankees?"

"Even the Yankees. And even if the boy wants it. What boy doesn't want the Yankees? But he's worth a lot more than forty thousand. Don't settle for less than six figures."

I was playing stickball with Tony Tiska and a couple of other guys on the fair grounds across the street from the house when Ray Garland drove up. Dad came out to meet him and yelled over for me to go in, and as I left the kids I couldn't help saying, "That's the Yankee scout. I'm going to sign with the Yankees today." Then, with a big grin on my face, I walked across the street and into the house.

He knows what we want, I thought, *and now he'll offer it. Otherwise, why would he come all the way out to see us? And*

*when he makes the offer Dad will accept it. I know he will. And
then I'll be a Yankee.*

Ray shook hands with me, and we all sat down in the living
room—Mom, Dad, Ray, and I. Ray pulled out a sheaf of contracts and a pen and a couple of pencils and a pad of scratch paper and looked at each one of us. Then he said, "Mr. MacPhail
has authorized me to raise the offer."

I took a long breath and glanced over at Dad. His face was
impassive.

"I'll tell you what I'm going to do," Ray said.

Here it comes.

"Mr. MacPhail," Ray said, "has told me to go to forty-five
thousand."

I let my breath out and looked at Dad. His expression hadn't
changed.

"What do you think, Carl?" Garland was addressing my father, not me.

Dad didn't say anything.

Ray pulled the scratch pad over and began writing figures on
it. "The Yankees win the pennant almost every year," he said.
"That's eight, ten thousand more from the World Series over
and above salary."

He looked at Dad, and Dad looked flatly back at him.

"He's a great young prospect," Ray said, tearing a sheet
off the scratch pad and writing down more figures. "He won't
be in the minors more than a couple of years, and when he comes
up he'll make it big. In five years he'll be up around fifty thousand a year."

Dad didn't move.

"The way he can hit," Ray said, tearing another sheet off
the scratch pad and scribbling as he talked, "he might be the
next great Yankee star, and you know what that means. In ten
years he'll be making a hundred thousand, maybe more."

He paused. There wasn't a sound in the room. Then he tore
still another sheet from the scratch pad and said, "There's no
limit to what he can make, with all the extras and everything.

And New York is the place for it—the big advertising and promotion market. He'll be good for a quarter of a million dollars a year."

He looked over at Dad again, but he might as well have been looking at the wall. Dad simply stared back at him, not speaking, not frowning, not smiling, not doing anything, just sitting there.

I couldn't stand it any longer. "Okay, okay," I exploded. "Give me the contract. I'll sign it."

Ray smiled and said, "See, Carl, your boy understands. He wants the Yankees, don't you, son?"

"You bet I want the Yankees," I said. "Please, Dad."

"What do you think, Carl?" Ray said.

Dad tore the top sheet off the scratch pad and in huge, thick figures wrote right across all Ray's scribbling, "100,000," pushed the sheet back to Ray, and quietly said, "That's what it will cost you to get him."

The scout reached across the table, scooped up all the sheets and the pencils and the contracts and the scratch paper, and threw them high in the air. As they floated down, landing all over the living room, I remember thinking, *There goes the Yankees,* and Ray Garland said, "The Yankees never offered that kind of money to anybody, and they won't give it to your boy."

"Then they'll never get him," Dad said.

"You're asking too much money, Carl," Ray said.

"Nobody will get my son for less," Dad said.

Although disappointed, I wasn't terribly upset. Both Dad and Father Joe were certain that sooner or later somebody would offer what we wanted. The word got around quickly that we had turned the Yankees down, but that didn't stop scouts—including Ray Garland—from continuing to watch me in Lake Ronkonkoma games and any others I played in. However, nobody approached us with other concrete offers that year and we didn't look for any. It wasn't until the following summer, after I returned home from my freshman year at Notre Dame, that we began hearing directly from scouts or ball clubs. And when we did, the action was fast and furious.

Practically all of it took place at Lake Ronkonkoma when Dad and I went down there to play. Not long after I got back from South Bend, Honey Russell of the Milwaukee Braves talked to us there with Whit Wyatt, the Braves' pitching coach. Honey was an old friend of ours who had followed my career since the Babe Ruth League. We had never met Wyatt, but had heard of him, for he was one of the best-known teachers and judges of young pitchers in baseball.

"Carl," Honey said to Dad, "we're prepared to make you a very attractive offer."

"Go ahead," Dad said.

"We'll give your boy sixty thousand dollars to sign with us as a pitcher," Russell said.

"Nothing doing," Dad said. "He's not available for sixty thousand, and if he were it wouldn't be as a pitcher."

"He could be one of the best pitchers in baseball," Wyatt said. "I'd like to work with him."

"I know your reputation and I know you'd do well by him," Dad said. "But my son is too good a hitter to pitch."

Shortly after that we heard from Frank (Chick) Genovese of the Giants, who had just shifted their franchise from New York to San Francisco. He didn't talk money because Dad didn't give him a chance to.

"I've seen this boy catch," Genovese said, "and good catchers are hard to come by. We'll match or top any offer he gets if he'll come with us."

"No thanks," Dad said. "He doesn't want to go to the West Coast, and if he did it wouldn't be as a catcher."

There were so many scouts, farm directors, and even general managers looking at New York and Long Island ballplayers that summer that a doubleheader for their convenience was arranged between a couple of all-star teams, and I was invited to play for one of them. The games didn't mean very much, but I had a fantastic afternoon—three homers, seven hits in eight times up, and a perfect day in the field. After that the phone in our house never stopped ringing.

Although scouts were always out at the house, Bots Nekola of the Red Sox, was the only one who ever took us all out to dinner and who made us feel that he was really interested in us. He never tried to pressure us into signing. I liked Bots, a big, friendly Holy Cross College graduate who had once pitched for the Yankees and whom Dad faced several times when he pitched for the Bushwicks. I was always so comfortable and at home with him that I hoped some day we would sign with the Red Sox, and he was a big factor in our eventual decision to do so. In the meantime, we talked to everybody who talked to us.

One night at Lake Ronkonkoma, Tommy Holmes of the Dodgers came around with Al Campanis, their director of scouts. After a lengthy discussion Campanis said, "We'll match or top any offer you get."

He took us by surprise for a minute; then Dad said, almost to himself, "If you were only still in Brooklyn."

But they weren't in Brooklyn. Nobody around the New York area had yet got used to the fact that they had left, since that was the Dodgers' first year in Los Angeles, but there was no denying that they weren't the Brooklyn Dodgers any more. Dad told Holmes and Campanis I'd rather play in the East, and that was that.

We never went to Lake Ronkonkoma that we weren't approached by somebody. We saw Dave Hall of the Reds from time to time, and Pat Mullin of the Tigers, who sometimes was accompanied by his boss, Johnny McHale, their farm director. Dale Jones of the Phillies was a regular visitor, and through him we met Jimmy Gallagher, their director of scouts.

Nobody made any specific offers, and we didn't encourage any. Although I got sort of impatient as the summer wore on, Dad was in no hurry to make a deal. We had dozens of talks with Father Joe, who helped us narrow the choices down. He had good friends in baseball, men who could help him advise us and whose judgment he could trust.

"Why don't we sign with somebody, Dad?" I said. "I'm sure we can get what we want."

"Wait," he said. "We'll know better after we've checked on everyone."

So we waited, while I met one scout and farm director after another, talking in vague terms, never knowing for sure where to go or what to do. Then one day, just before I was to leave for my sophomore year at Notre Dame, Father Joe said, "I think your two best bets are the Phillies and the Red Sox. They're both in the East. They're both great organizations. Bob Carpenter of the Phillies and Tom Yawkey of the Red Sox are fine owners and known for their generosity to their ballplayers. If either will give you what you want, I think you should take it."

We phoned Jimmy Gallagher, who had given me an open invitation to work out in Philadelphia whenever I wanted to, and he told us to go down the next day. Then Dad called Tommy Skripps, a cousin of his from Long Island who had gone to college with Bob Carpenter and lived in Carpenter's home town of Wilmington, Delaware, where he managed the Continental Can plant. Uncle Tommy, still a close friend of Carpenter's, had always been interested in me and promised to see us at the ball park. Mom, Dad, and I drove to Philadelphia and checked in at the Hotel Warwick; then Dale Jones took Dad and me to the park. Gallagher greeted us warmly, escorted us to the locker room, and introduced us to Manager Eddie Sawyer, Richie Ashburn, Robin Roberts, and all the other Phillie ballplayers. When Dad and I were both given lockers right with them, I couldn't help thinking of that day in Yankee Stadium when they made me dress with the batboys.

Everyone went out of his way to be nice to us, including Chico Fernandez, the regular shortstop. A friendly Cuban, he came over to me on the field, shook hands, and with a big grin said in a heavy accent, "If you can beat me out for this job, good luck." Eddie Sawyer had a word of encouragement every time he went by me, and Wally Moses, the batting coach, hovered over me like a mother hen. While I was waiting to hit he never left me, and when I got ready to move into the batting cage he told me just to take my natural swing and not worry where the ball went.

"We know what you can do," he said. "If you don't do it here and now, it won't make a bit of difference."

But I did do it there and then. I stood in the batting cage, even looser and more confident than I had been at Yankee Stadium, and belted pitches all over the place—to left, to right, to center, into the stands in left center field, against and over the scoreboard in right. I took maybe fifty swings and must have hit fifteen balls out of the park. When I stepped out, Moses said, "Son, you're the finest young hitter I've ever seen." And Robin Roberts yelled to Fernandez, "See you later, Chico. This'll be *your* last year." And Chico grinned and waved to me.

While Dad and I were dressing, somebody said Bob Carpenter wanted to see me right away, and one of the coaches came over to us and said, "Get all you can. They're ready to pay." But we didn't see Carpenter right away. Instead, the two of us were taken to Jimmy Gallagher's office.

He talked a while about the virtues of playing for the Phillies, then said, "You're a great young prospect. We'll give you $60,000 to sign."

"If that's what you're thinking about, there's no sense talking any more," Dad said. "You know what we want—$100,000 and the rest of his college tuition."

"We'll give him a big-league contract," Gallagher said. "That's a minimum salary of seven thousand a year."

Dad just looked at him.

"Okay," Gallagher said, "we'll count this as a full season. We'll give him a whole year's salary for nineteen fifty-eight, even though the season's practically over."

"He's going back to college," Dad said.

"We'll put him in the line-up tonight," Gallagher said. "He can play against the Cubs."

Without a word Dad stood up.

"Sixty thousand is a lot of money," Gallagher said.

"Not enough," Dad said.

We had dinner with Mom and Uncle Tommy and went back

for the ball game, then made arrangements to see Carpenter the next day and went to bed.

Uncle Tommy and Jimmy Gallagher were in Carpenter's office when Dad and I got there.

"We want you to play for the Phillies," Carpenter said. After talking a while he said, "We'll give you $80,000."

This was the highest offer yet, and I remember thinking maybe it was the highest offer we'd get. I looked at Dad, half hoping he'd say yes, but the minute I saw his eyes I knew he wouldn't. He was giving Carpenter that blank stare.

"I know you want a hundred, Mr. Yastrzemski," Carpenter said, "but look at the tax you'll have to pay."

He took out a pen and paper and began figuring aloud. I couldn't follow him, and I'm sure Dad couldn't either, because he was talking a language neither of us understood.

". . . so you see," he said, "you'll really end up the same way with $80,000 as you would with $100,000. What do you think, Mr. Yastrzemski?"

"I think we want a hundred thousand and the rest of his tuition," Dad said.

"The government will take an awful income-tax bite out of that," Carpenter said.

Dad just sat and stared. Then Uncle Tommy said, "Now, Bob, there's no sense talking about income taxes. You can come up with all the tax advantages you want to out of $80,000 and show that it's the same or better than $100,000, but there's only one thing that will make the old man sign: in plain, simple English, $100,000. And if you want this boy, that's what it's got to be."

"Plus the rest of his college expenses," Dad said.

After some discussion and figuring and income-tax talk, Carpenter finally said, "Okay, we'll give you $95,000."

I sucked in my breath. This was closer to $100,000 than I had ever really hoped to get, and I thought sure Dad would take it. But he made no move, and the expression on his face was still blank.

"We'll give him a big-league contract," Carpenter said. "That's another $7000, and with the season almost over, it's like a bonus of $102,000."

Dad was weakening. He leaned forward, drummed his fingers on the table, then suddenly said, "Let me think about it."

"Isn't that the bonus you want?" Carpenter said.

"I'm tired," Dad said. "I'd rather wait until tomorrow."

"Okay," Carpenter said, standing up. "We'll talk tomorrow."

We talked at length at dinner that night. Uncle Tommy, eager for me to play in Philadelphia, tried to talk Dad into accepting Carpenter's last offer, but Dad still insisted on my college expenses. And the next day, that was the first thing he brought up in Carpenter's office.

"I've been thinking about that," Carpenter said. "I've set up a scholarship fund at the University of Delaware. If Carl goes there on a semester basis, we'll pay all of his expenses out of that."

"Plus the $102,000?" Dad said.

"That's right."

"Okay," Dad said. "I'll go along with that. There's just one other thing. He's got one year of college behind him. To get a degree, he'll have to go six more semesters, which will take him six years because he can't go any second semesters on account of baseball. Who knows what might happen in six years? Maybe he'll quit college before he finishes. If he does, you give him another $10,000."

"What if it's his senior year?" Carpenter said.

"Any year," Dad said. "If he quits before he gets his degree, you pay him $10,000."

"Mr. Yastrzemski," Carpenter said, "you asked for $100,000, and we're offering the equivalent of $102,000. You asked for the rest of his college expenses, and we're offering to pay them. I think that's as far as you can expect us to go. If your son decides to quit college before he finishes, that has nothing to do with us and there's no reason it should cost us $10,000."

We argued most of the day about it, and at dinner that night

Uncle Tommy said to Dad, "Carl, you upped your price, of course."

"That's right," Dad said.

"I think you ought to sign without that $10,000 stipulation."

"If sonny goes one semester and quits, look at all the money Carpenter will save," Dad said.

"If he goes to his senior year and quits, why should it cost Carpenter $10,000?" Uncle Tommy said.

"I don't care when he quits," Dad said. "He's got to get $10,-000 if he quits."

That was the way Dad wanted it, and that was the way it stayed. We spent another day with Carpenter, but neither he nor Dad gave an inch. When we finally stood up to go, Carpenter shook hands all around, then said to me, "Carl, here's my telephone credit-card number. Call anywhere you want any time you want." Then, turning to Dad, he said, "Our offer still stands —$102,000 plus the rest of his college expenses. Let me know if you decide to take it."

Back home we had a call from Bots Nekola asking us to go to Boston, but it was too late, because I had to be at Notre Dame the next day. Between then and late November Dad and I had periodic phone calls and wires, mostly from the Red Sox, and Dad agreed to go to Boston with me during Thanksgiving vacation. At that point I was sure that if the Red Sox didn't satisfy us we'd accept the Phillies' offer. It never occurred to me that anyone else would be interested, at our price.

About two weeks before Thanksgiving the Cincinnati Reds unexpectedly came into the picture. Dave Hall, their Long Island scout, had never indicated any willingness to talk six figures to us, but Gabe Paul, their general manager, phoned Dad, told him the Reds knew what we wanted and would give it to us. Then Paul went to Bridgehampton to see him and Mom over the weekend, while his assistant, Paul Florence, came to South Bend to see me. After dinner Friday night we went to my room to take a prearranged phone call from home.

Gabe Paul talked first, telling me the Reds wanted me

so badly that he had checks totaling $100,000 all ready to give Dad, that he'd give me a major-league contract and a chance to break right into the line-up the following spring, that the Cincinnati ball park was made for me and I was made for it, and so forth. Then he left the room in Bridgehampton and Florence went out of my room, so Dad and I could talk privately.

"He wants to give me $100,000 in five checks of $20,000 each," Dad said. "And he promised to pay the rest of your way through college."

"What did you tell him?" I asked.

"I said it wasn't enough money."

"What did you ask for?"

Dad laughed. "I didn't ask for anything," he said. "I just wrote a figure down and handed it to him."

"How much?" I said.

"A hundred fifty thousand."

I gulped, which I imagined was what Gabe Paul must have done.

"Don't tell me he offered it," I said.

"He offered $125,000," Dad said. "That's where we are now. What do you think?"

"I don't know because I've never seen the Cincinnati ball park," I said.

"Okay," Dad said. "Let's leave it open until we get out there. Detroit wants to talk to us too. When we pick you up in South Bend for Thanksgiving vacation, we'll drive to Detroit and Cincinnati and then go to Boston."

After we hung up I realized something I had never thought of before. My dad, a poor potato farmer all his life, a man who never knew how things would go for him and had never seen $10,000 in one year in his life, was getting a tremendous charge out of just talking in terms of huge sums of money. He was the little man making the big man look foolish, the underdog whipping the favorite, the 100-to-1 shot upsetting all the odds, David killing one Goliath after another.

And I realized something else—that even though he knew he

would turn the Reds down unless they went to $150,000, he wanted to talk some more with Gabe Paul just to roll all those big figures off his tongue. He wanted to know how high Paul would go, where Paul would draw the line, when he would say no. And, in a way, he had done the very same thing with Bob Carpenter, for the club he really wanted was the Red Sox because of Bots Nekola, whom we both liked very much. As long as it was in six figures, Dad would take less from the Red Sox than from anyone, and would turn to the Phillies only if the Red Sox failed to go up that high.

We saw Johnny McHale at Detroit. Formerly the farm director, he had just been made general manager of the Tigers.

"We know what you want," McHale said. "And I'm sure we can give it to you when the time comes. But the most we can offer right now is $80,000 because we're in a transitional period. The Briggs family is selling the club to a syndicate headed by John Fetzer, but the deal hasn't been completed yet."

"Will Mr. Fetzer be the sole owner?" Dad asked.

"No."

"Thanks, but we're not interested," Dad said. "We want a club with a single owner or a family ownership."

From Detroit we headed for Cincinnati to see if Gabe Paul would meet our $150,000 figure. He was very nice, but flatly refused to go higher than $125,000 plus college expenses. It wasn't enough for Dad. After turning down the best offer we had (and the best we could get), Dad and I shook hands with Paul, said good-by, and left.

In Boston, two days later, we checked into the old Kenmore Hotel around the corner from Fenway Park (it's a school now) and started dickering with Johnny Murphy, the farm director, with Bots sitting in. His first offer was $100,000 plus tuition. Dad countered with a demand for $125,000, but I could see his heart wasn't in it. He didn't have his patented blank stare and he didn't sit and say nothing. He liked Bots and he liked Murphy and he wanted me to play for the Red Sox and knew I wanted to. If the Red Sox wouldn't spring for $125,000, Dad would settle for less.

We didn't settle anything that first day. That night Bots and Johnny took us all to dinner at Stella's, and the next day we went back to Fenway Park. When Murphy asked him what he thought, Dad said, "We'll take $115,000." We talked a few minutes; then Murphy said, "We'll give you $108,000, plus a two-year Triple A farm contract at $5000 a year, plus the rest of your college expenses."

"Well, son," Dad said, "what do you think?"

"I'm satisfied," I said. "How about you?"

"I'm ready to sign," he said.

Just after we signed and were about to leave for home, Joe Cronin, then the club's general manager, came in and said, "I want to meet the boy we're giving all this money to."

As we shook hands, he took in my 5-feet-11, 170-pound frame, then turned to Murphy and said, "He doesn't seem very big."

"He hits big, Joe," Murphy said.

"Okay," Cronin said. Turning to me, he said, "You must really swing that bat." Then he walked out, shaking his head like a man who had met a midget when he expected a giant.

The same thing happened to me when I got my regular allowance check from Dad at Notre Dame the next week. As usual, it was for $5.00. I rushed to the phone, called him collect and said, "Damn, Pop, after the contract I just signed, I think I ought to get more than five bucks a week. How about a raise?"

"Okay," he said.

The next week he sent me $7.50. And that was my allowance for the rest of the semester.

CHAPTER 5

Carol

I didn't like Notre Dame at first. Worried about Grandpa Skonieczny, lonesome for home, buried in a highly disciplined university atmosphere, trying to get by on my Dad's $5-a-week allowance, resentful that he hadn't let me take one of those fat financial offers from the South, I could think of plenty of places I'd rather be than South Bend. If it hadn't been for Father Boarman and my pals Bernie Dobransky from Pittsburgh and Ron Zak from Toledo, I wouldn't have lasted a month.

As prefect of religion at Breen Phillips Hall, Father Boarman met incoming freshmen on registration day. He did what he could to make me feel at home then and later. Realizing how unhappy I was, he tried to help me adjust to campus life. He cushioned the shock of Grandpa Skonieczny's death only a few weeks after I entered college. He helped me with my studies, which were tougher than any I had ever had in high school. He talked baseball by the hour and encouraged me in my professional ambitions. And he made himself available to me whenever I felt I needed him, which was often.

Through Father Boarman, Bernie, Ron, and I were invited

right after Thanksgiving to a mixer at Saint Mary's, a swanky Catholic girls' school in South Bend. I had just become interested in girls during my senior year in high school and welcomed the chance to meet a few. The trouble was, Saint Mary's girls had so much money that I didn't belong on the same dance floor with them—if, in view of my horrible dancing, I belonged on any dance floor with anybody.

While I was stumbling around trying to dance with a girl at the mixer, she asked what my parents were giving me for Christmas.

"A bathrobe," I said, knowing I needed one. "And other stuff I can use at college."

"Like what?" she said.

"A suit," I said. I wasn't getting a suit, but I had to tell her something. "Two suits," I said, warming up to the subject. "Maybe three. And a couple of pairs of shoes—alligator shoes. And a dozen monogrammed shirts. And—uh—slacks and sports jackets and sports shirts and an overcoat and—"

"And what?"

"A television set," I said. "And a movie camera and projector."

"Is that all?"

"What are you getting?" I said.

"I'm pretty mad at my dad," she said. "All he's giving me is a Corvette."

"What did you expect?"

"He promised me an oil well," she said.

I excused myself, hunted up Bernie and Ron, and said, "Come on. Let's get out of here. This is no place for three poor Polish kids like us."

Later I started going with a Saint Mary's girl from New Orleans who invited me to Mardi Gras week. Father Boarman told me her father was a multimillionaire doctor with more oil wells than he knew what to do with. It all sounded like a pretty good deal, except that the nearer we came to Mardi Gras week the colder my feet got. I didn't dare tell the girl my old man was a poor potato farmer, especially when she took it for granted that all I had to do to hop down to New Orleans was ask him for the money and go. The only way I could get out of it was pick a fight with her. We broke up two weeks before the Mardi Gras, and I never saw her again.

One of the first things I learned at Notre Dame was how to play bridge. I didn't know much about cards up to then—barely knew the suits—but I learned fast. At one point we played bridge just about every waking hour when we weren't studying. I mentioned bridge so often in letters home that my mother finally said, "Is that what you're at college for, to play bridge? Haven't you learned anything else?"

Bernie and Ron and I couldn't do much else on the budgets we were on. The three of us considered it a big night when we went downtown for a spaghetti dinner and a movie. There was a place in South Bend where you could get a whole meal for a dollar and a quarter. The three of us would go there for the spaghetti special and fill up on bread, which came with the dinner. We'd get bread by the basket—maybe ten baskets a meal. With more customers like us, the guy who ran the place would have gone broke in a week.

It was through Bernie that I met my wife, Carol Casper, who had gone to school with him. She was a receptionist for the Pittsburgh branch of a big oil company, but that was the nearest to oil wells she ever got. Her father was a salesman, making not much more money than my dad averaged raising potatoes.

Right after I signed my Red Sox contract, Bernie invited me home to Pittsburgh for the weekend and set up a blind date for me with Carol. Since everything I owned was on paper, I didn't have enough cash for the trip and entertainment expenses, so I borrowed $60 from Father Boarman. One look at Carol, and I was hooked. She is a stunning blonde with a warm, friendly manner, and her first words to me were, "Anyone with a name like Yastrzemski has to be a winner." Before the evening was over I asked her—only half in fun—to marry me.

Bernie and Carol's closest friend, Pat Snyder, went out with us that first night. With Father Boarman's money burning a hole in my pocket, I said, "I've just signed this nice big baseball contract. Let's have a celebration." We went to the Twin Coaches, a night club where Eydie Gorme was singing, and the first thing I ordered was a bottle of champagne. While it was on the way I noticed there was a $5.00 cover charge per couple, but I still felt like the last of the big spenders.

"Order whatever you want, girls," I said.

When they both ordered steaks, figures began flashing through my mind: $6.50 per steak, $13.00; champagne, $20.00; cover charge, $10.00—that was $43.00, which was getting pretty close to what I had in my pocket. Before Bernie could order, I said to the waiter, "I'll have some chicken," and Bernie said, "So will I." Chicken was $2.75—$5.50 on top of the $43.00 would leave me enough for a tip.

Since Carol said she loved to dance, I went out on the floor with her, but we hadn't been there two minutes before she said, "You're the worst dancer I ever saw. Maybe we'd better go back to the table and talk." That was exactly what I wanted to do anyhow, so I had a marvelous evening. The next day we went sightseeing in trolley cars, and that night to a movie. The day after that I had dinner at her house and we made dates for the following weekend and were openly talking, still only half kidding, about getting married.

Although Carol's parents and Suzanne, her eleven-year-old sister, were hot Pittsburgh Pirate fans, Carol knew practically nothing about baseball. Her sister had been studying box scores and sports pages since she was seven, but Carol wouldn't even bother to look when the family had the Pirates on television. Suzanne and her parents went to Forbes Field to watch ball games whenever they could, but Carol had never been there in her life up to the time she met me. All she knew about baseball was that when the ball goes over the fence it's a home run. Suzanne, who knew all about the bonus the Red Sox had given me, was much more impressed with me than Carol was.

Although we had known each other only a few weeks, Carol went to Bridgehampton to meet my relatives during the first part of my Christmas vacation. She and Grandma Skonieczny became very close, as, indeed, they still are. We spent the last part of the vacation in Pittsburgh, but Carol couldn't break a long-standing date for New Year's Eve. I took Suzanne to the movies while swearing I'd never take Carol out New Year's Eve, but that was one resolution I didn't keep.

The following May, when I was playing for Raleigh, I got permission from Johnny Murphy to fly to Pittsburgh and spend Carol's birthday with her. That time I was loaded—I had about $1000 in cash with me—and I wanted to get her something real nice. I spent the night at her house; then we went downtown in the trolley to a jeweler's, where I was going to buy Carol a pair of expensive rosaries she said she'd like. In the trolley I said, "This is a good day for us to get engaged."

"Okay," she said in the same light vein we always used when we talked about marriage.

"Well, I mean it," I said.

She peered hard at me, then said, "You do, don't you?"

So instead of the rosaries we decided to buy a diamond ring. When the guy at the jewelry shop asked how much I wanted to spend, I said somewhere between $500 and $1000. Carol picked one out for about $700, but when I reached for my wallet I had only about $100.

"I'll have to go back and get it," I said.

"That's okay," the clerk said. "You can give me a check. Just give me some identification."

"Look," I said, turning to Carol, "you stay here and I'll go back and get the money. It'll only take about twenty minutes."

So Carol stayed in the shop while I took a trolley to her house, got the money, rode back to town, and paid the guy cash for the diamond. That night we told her folks, and I phoned mine.

That was easy, for my parents liked Carol and hers liked me. But selling my folks the idea of our getting married where and when we wanted to was something else again. Not wanting a long engagement, we decided on a January 1960 wedding in Raleigh, where I had played the year before. We picked Raleigh because it was the only place that meant anything to us where banns didn't have to be published in the Catholic church three weeks in advance. Neither Carol nor I could spare that much time.

Her parents were agreeable to our getting married so soon, but mine raised the roof. Our ages—we were only twenty—was one objection, but there were others. They were worried that I might not finish college and that marriage before I had made it to the Red Sox might affect my career. Carol came to Bridgehampton for New Year's, and the two of us did everything we could to talk them into accepting our plan, but they wouldn't hear of it. Father Joe, who agreed with us, came over several times, but he couldn't budge them either. We finally decided that we would get married anyhow and told them so, while promising faithfully that I would finish college, if not at Notre Dame, then somewhere. And on the day we left, Carol for home and I for South Bend, they finally consented.

Father Boarman married us in a formal ceremony far different from the Polish weddings of my youth. We had about a hundred guests, keeping the list down to relatives no farther removed than first cousins. Carol's came down from Pittsburgh and mine from Long Island for a big party the night before at a motel in Raleigh which we practically took over. The wedding itself was simple. After the marriage Mass there was a meal with a lot of toasting to the bride and groom, and not very much else. We didn't even have any dancing, since the groom would have made a fool of himself trying to guide the bride around the floor. We honeymooned at Sea Island, Georgia, then flew to Scottsdale, Arizona, where the Red Sox trained at the time.

I had a good spring training, but off the field life wasn't very pleasant for either of us. There was some resentment on the part of other ballplayers because of my bonus, which, although never guessed accurately by the press, had been highly publicized as being over $100,000. Carol, extremely popular in her home town and now away from it permanently for the first time, badly wanted friends and found it difficult to make any. So, for that matter, did I. At Raleigh my closest friend had been Chuck Schilling, a Long Island boy who had been our second baseman, but he was in Deland, Florida, with Minneapolis, then the top Red Sox farm club.

At Scottsdale we stayed at the Imperial Apartments with many of the other married Red Sox ballplayers, but the only people who paid any attention to us were Amy and Frank Malzone. They were considerably older and probably felt sorry for a couple of lonesome kids. If they hadn't, we would have spent the whole spring-training period all by ourselves. Nobody but the Malzones ever asked us anywhere, not even to join them for dinner. Nobody but Amy talked to Carol, and nobody but Frank spoke to me off the field.

It was such an unhappy experience that it took us both years to forget it, if, indeed, we ever really did. Because of that dreadful spring, I never found it easy to fraternize with teammates. Although I got along all right with everybody, the only truly close friend I have ever had on the Red Sox ball club was Schilling, my roommate when he played for us. Except for him, I was always a bit of a loner, which is not my nature at all. I would have been more gregarious, friendlier, and much happier if it hadn't been for the deep freeze in which Carol and I lived during those first few weeks of our marriage. We have both been grateful to the Malzones ever since. While we don't get together often, Amy and Carol are still good friends, and so are Frank and I.

Our family life has always been blighted by travel. Since the day we met we have always had to go somewhere to be together —to Pittsburgh, to South Bend, to Bridgehampton before we were married, and all over the place later. Carol once counted twenty-seven moves in a year—it must have been around 1961 or 1962, after Maryann and Mike, our two older children, were born. But we did plenty of traveling even before they arrived. After Scottsdale, the year we were married, I went to Deland to join the Minneapolis club, and Carol drove home to Pittsburgh with my parents, who had joined us in Arizona. She met me in Minneapolis, where we lived during the 1960 baseball season, but of course I was home only half the time. Then we went to South Bend, and from there Carol went to Pittsburgh for the birth of Maryann in the fall of 1960. After that we sort of commuted between Pittsburgh, South Bend, and Bridgehampton until it was time to report to Scottsdale for spring training.

We finally reached Boston for good in 1961. I had been in and out of there several times by then and had fallen in love with the city and its surroundings. So did Carol. Knowing this was where we intended to make our home, we bought a house in 1962 in Lynnfield, not far from where we now live.

Before that I tried to continue at Notre Dame, but it became too much of a chore. Carol and I lived there for two first semesters, in 1960 and 1961. By then we had both Maryann and Mike—Suzann, our third, wasn't born until 1966—and returning to Notre Dame every year meant that many more extra moves. It wasn't simply going to South Bend at the beginning of the semester and leaving at the end, but traveling to Pittsburgh or Bridgehampton for vacations and even weekends that drove us nuts. We had hoped to stay put after baseball seasons, but instead we seemed to be moving around more than ever.

After buying our first house in Lynnfield, I decided to finish my studies at Merrimack College, a Catholic school run by the Augustinian fathers in North Andover. I picked it out partly because they would integrate my courses with what I had taken at Notre Dame and partly because it was a reasonable commute from Lynnfield and I could go there without getting messed up in city traffic.

Getting into Merrimack was no problem. But getting out with a degree was something else again. I had so many other things to do that it was a real chore making it to classes. Fortunately I was allowed unlimited cuts and could make up much of the work with outside reading, but often I hardly had time for that. I would have thrown in the towel after one year if it hadn't been for my promise to my folks. I had told them I'd get a degree, if not at Notre Dame then somewhere else, and I wouldn't quit until I had it. But a Red Sox ballplayer living in Greater

Boston is always pretty busy in the winter. The ball club didn't load you up with banquets, but they expected you to make a few, and you never knew when something unexpected might come up.

I went to classes when I had time or when I hadn't been up half the night before on the banquet circuit. Professor Tom Hogan, head of the Economics Department and an especially close friend of mine, used to phone in the morning and say, "Carl, are you coming in today?"

"If I can," I'd say.

"Well," Tom would say, "try and make it."

If it hadn't been for him I would never have got through. I wasn't stupid, but I went to class so seldom people used to greet me with handshakes because they hadn't seen me for so long. Before the day was over, I'd be in Tom's office for help in catching up on what I missed, or he'd promise to come around to the house to give me a hand. I think he made my house more often than I made his college.

Father Wesson was another faculty member who gave me a big hand. Like Tom Hogan, he called from time to time to beg me to show up for class, and I always told him I would if I could. And, like Tom, he spent hours with me, helping me catch up or getting me ready for exams. The professors, who understood my problems, were all very cooperative.

Besides being with the Red Sox (Tom and Father Wesson were ardent baseball fans), I had one thing going for me. Whether I made classes or not, I was always good at cramming for exams. When exam time came around, Tom would take me to see the professor of a class I had spent most of the semester missing and say, "What notes does he have to do?"

The answer was usually, "The whole course." And the man would then produce pages and pages for me to read. I'd take the stuff home and study for a couple of days and nights without much sleep, then hit the exam on the nose. The only A's I got were for absenteeism, but I never flunked anything and, based on the exams, my passing grades were on the level.

I was due to get my degree in February of 1966, but first I had to pass a tough philosophy course given by Dr. John Warren. He was a nice guy and very understanding about my not appearing at class, but he told Tom and me that he didn't see how I could possibly pass the intensive final he intended to give in a few days.

"Carl is very good at cramming," Tom said. "Do you suppose you could give him your notes to study?"

"I'll be glad to," said Dr. Warren, "but I doubt if they'll help much. This is the kind of course that has to be explained to be understood."

I took the notes anyhow and went home to work on them. I really beat my brains out for a couple of days, but the stuff was all too deep for me. By the time I was through I had no more idea what the guy meant about God and man and all that jazz than when I started. I finally went to Father Wesson the afternoon before the exam and said, "What do I do now? I've got a final in philosophy tomorrow and I don't know a thing about it."

"Okay," Father Wesson said. "The best mind we've got in college and maybe in the whole Augustinian order is Father Burt. Let's see if he'll help you."

Father Burt was head of the Philosophy Department and had exams of his own to correct, but he was a Red Sox fan too. When he heard that I couldn't get my degree without passing this course he said, "All right. Let's get to work."

We worked on the notes for nine solid hours, from four in the afternoon until one in the morning, and I finally had them down cold. Then Father Burt said, "Review them in your head on the way home. Think of them before you go to sleep. And get out of here, please. I've got tests of my own to correct before I go to bed." I wonder if he got to bed at all that night.

I retained all that stuff he crammed into my head just long enough to pour it out on the exam the next day, and I don't mind telling you I hit it hard. When Tom told me a day or two later, "You got a C," I said, "I thought I deserved a B," and he broke up. Except for the first one and the last, I hadn't been to a philosophy class all semester.

Anyhow, I graduated, and Mom and Dad and Carol and Father Wesson and Tom were happy as could be. Rich had already got his degree from LaSalle, and when I got mine Dad shook hands with me and said, "Now both my sons have college educations."

When the Red Sox won the 1967 pennant, Merrimack College stretched a sign 200 feet long across the road in front of the main gate, which read: YAZ WENT TO SCHOOL HERE. Later Father Wesson told me that he and Tom took one look at that thing and felt like putting another sign beneath it. That one would read: THE HELL HE DID.

CHAPTER 6

Life in the Minors

Although they signed me as a shortstop, the Red Sox made a second baseman out of me because that was where they thought I'd be needed most by the time I worked my way up through the farm system. They were satisfied with Don Buddin, their regular shortstop, who was only twenty-five, but second base had been a problem for years. The shift didn't bother me. I had played enough second base in semi-pro ball to know the fundamentals of the job.

But at Raleigh, where I broke into professional baseball in 1959, I got off to a frighteningly slow start. In the first two weeks of a 130-game season I hit only .240, didn't have a single homer, and fielded sluggishly. The bat felt heavier and the ball looked smaller every day. Worrying and wondering if all my dreams were going up in smoke, I tossed around in bed, and even my normally big appetite was affected.

Then I realized that my only trouble was getting used to a strange new way of life. For the first time I was living as a ballplayer, not as a farm boy with ambitions to become a ballplayer. Baseball was now my business, something I had to do every day, something I could never get away from. A semi-pro plays when he wants to and doesn't when he doesn't. A pro plays whether he wants to or not.

At Raleigh we played five nights a week and Sunday afternoons. I had rarely played more than twice a week nights and once a week days, and never on a compulsory basis. And whether I played in the daytime or at night, I had never changed my routine of getting up early in the morning, eating on a regular schedule, and going to bed at a reasonable hour at night during the week. Now I had to eat and sleep at crazy hours—breakfast at eleven in the morning, a big meal in midafternoon, a snack at midnight or later, bed sometimes as late as two in the morning, depending on where we played and how long it took to get back.

Bus travel, an unwelcome novelty to me, was an integral part of life in a Class B league. Ours, the Carolina League, was so compact that we never had to spend a night away from Raleigh, but we always seemed to be coming or going. I heard backfiring and bus wheels and gears grinding in my sleep, and stumbling down bus steps while the rest of Raleigh slept became routine.

All this took getting used to, and when I finally managed, I was a new man and a new ballplayer. Fast balls stopped handcuffing me, curve balls stopped fooling me, pitchers were human again, and the ball began looking more like a melon than a grape. When I started hitting, my fielding picked up, and pretty soon I was in a groove where I found everything I did a pleasure instead of a chore.

I even liked chores. When we played at home, I always tried to get extra batting practice if I hadn't felt good at the plate during the game. It didn't matter how many hits I collected that night. The hits were fine, but if I didn't feel loose and easy I knew I had to work my way out of it that very night. Taking extra batting practice after ball games in which my swing didn't feel right became a habit which has lasted to this day. I even did it after going hitless against Bob Gibson of the Cardinals in the first game of the 1967 World Series.

We won the Carolina League pennant, and I was the batting

champion with a .377 average. The runner-up was more than fifty points behind me. It was the highest average in that league in eleven years, and it won me the Most Valuable Player and Rookie-of-the-Year awards. I had only 15 home runs, but fences were pretty far out and I didn't have much to aim for. About half the homers were in Raleigh, where it was nearly 400 feet from the plate to right field.

Just before our season ended on September 11, the manager, Ken Deal, said, "Carl, you're going to Minneapolis. Mauch asked for you to help them out in the playoffs."

Minneapolis, managed by Gene Mauch, was the top Red Sox farm club, in the Class Triple A American Association.

"That's great," I said.

"You won't be eligible to play for a few days," Deal said, "so the Red Sox want you to stop in Boston on the way."

"In Boston?"

"They want to look at you and give you a chance to hit in Fenway Park."

The only time I had ever been in Boston was when I had signed my contract, and that was in November. Now I would see the ball park under game conditions, have a locker, even if only for a day, right with the big club, and maybe meet Ted Williams.

I flew to Boston the day after the Carolina League season ended. The trip was great and I felt fine all the way up, but in the hotel, just before walking around the corner to the ball park, I had a brief but intense attack of the jitters. My heart pounded and my stomach muscles tightened and gremlins ran up and down my spine as I packed my spiked shoes, my glove, and my sweatshirt. I finally got them into a bag, took the elevator down to the lobby, and headed for Fenway Park.

I felt better as I neared the place. *I'm almost part of this ball club now,* I thought. *They'll give me a big greeting after that year I had in Raleigh. I hope they give me a locker near Ted Williams. I'll surely meet him. I wonder what he'll say to me. And if the manager will say anything. If I hit a couple out of there, maybe they'll let me stay instead of sending me to Minneapolis.*

Still dreaming of hitting a couple out of there, I went to the players' gate.

"My name's Carl Yastrzemski," I said.

"They told me you were coming," the attendant said. "You know how to get to the locker room?"

I shook my head, and he gave me directions. I walked by the concessions headquarters beneath the grandstand, past a huge baseball with slots carrying names of Red Sox ballplayers, which I stopped to examine. There was a sign, "Give to the Jimmy Fund in the name of your favorite," and I thought, *my name will be there soon.* The Jimmy Fund, with which the Red Sox have been closely associated for years, raises money for children's-cancer research.

It was early when I arrived in the locker room, and there were only a few players, none of whom I recognized. As I walked in, Johnny Orlando, the equipment man, said, "You're Yastrzemski, aren't you? Your locker's over there somewhere." Without shaking hands, he waved an arm in the general direction of a line of lockers against the wall, then turned and walked away.

Scared, mad, uncomfortable, I watched him go to the opposite side of the clubhouse, into the corner which I learned later was Ted Williams' domain. Orlando was famous in baseball as Williams' close friend and personal equipment man. According to reports, Williams gave Orlando his share of the 1946 World Series receipts as a tip—a story that long since has become part of the Williams legend.

When Orlando disappeared through a door beside Williams' two lockers and bat rack—it led into a storeroom—I turned to look for my spot but found nothing except a line of perhaps half a dozen lockers, mostly empty or containing small items of equipment. But there was nothing with my name on it, or with a uniform in it, or with anything else a stranger might need to get ready for a workout. With no idea of what to do next, I picked a locker at random, sat on the stool in front of it, unpacked my spikes and glove and sweatshirt, and looked across at Williams' corner, where Orlando was now puttering around. I watched him go from one of Williams' two lockers to the other, lining up shoes and socks, straightening gleaming white uniforms, and seeing that all the other equipment was in its proper place.

I turned to other lockers nearer me. Directly across the section of the room where I sat was the line of lockers where my own is now located. Each contained equipment and uniform parts, all neatly arranged, the uniforms and sweatshirts on hangers, the shoes on racks, the gloves hanging by their straps, the stockings and inner socks lined up evenly.

The spiked shoes impressed me most. Each locker, with identifying names and numbers, had at least five pairs, and some had more. I looked down at my one beat-up old pair, which I used in dry weather and wet, in heat and in cold, in the field and at the plate. *What in the world do they do with five pairs of spikes?* I thought. *Why spend all that money? Oh, well, this is the big leagues. I guess that's the difference.*

I had been there perhaps ten minutes when a slight black-haired, blue-eyed youth, wearing white pants and a white shirt, and with a pixie face that looked like the map of Ireland, came into the room, spotted me, walked over, held out his hand, and said, "Hello, I'm Don Fitzpatrick."

"I'm Carl Yastrzemski."

"Yeah, sure, I know who you are," Fitzie said. "You're the kid who tore the Carolina League apart. Where's your uniform? You're going to work out, aren't you?"

"I guess I'm supposed to," I said. "But I don't have anything to work out in."

"What have you got of your own?"

"Just this," I said, pointing to the shoes and the glove and the sweatshirt.

"Is that all?" Fitzie said.

"That's all."

He picked up the sweatshirt, a cheap cotton one I had bought

Yaz's classic swing as he hits his
third home run in the 1967
World Series against the Cardinals.

Photos: Wide World

Yaz's batting tends to overshadow
his other talents. He is a first-class
base runner. Here he is beating a
force-out throw to second
against the California Angels.
Bobby Knoop is covering the bag.

Yaz has always been strong on the
bases. Here he is wreaking havoc
with the Yankee double-play
combination of Bobby Richardson
(right) and Tony Kubek. What's
more, he was safe.

Don't overlook his fielding skills,
either. Here he commits highway
robbery on a drive by Curt Flood in
the fifth game of the 1967
World Series.

Carl goes all out for a foul ball
hit by Lou Brock in the sixth
World Series game.

It was widely publicized after the
first World Series game that
Yaz often takes batting practice
immediately after a bad day at the
plate. Here's the proof.

Red Sox ace Jim Lonborg and Yaz
after the second World Series
game, in which Lonborg pitched a
one-hitter and Yaz hit two home
runs as the Red Sox won 5-0.

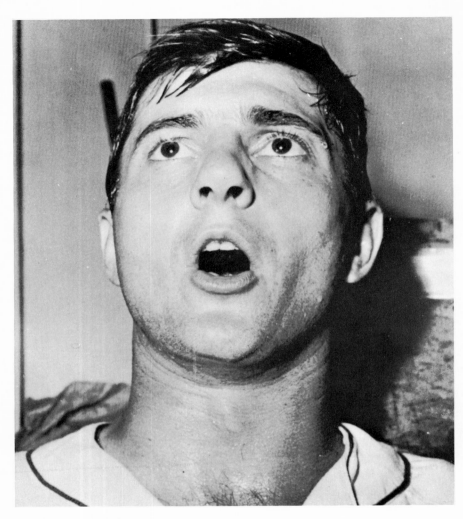

It took a long time but it was
worth the wait. It's great to
be a winner.

in Raleigh. It looked good down there, but now it seemed seedy and utterly inadequate.

"We'll get you a couple of new ones," Fitzie said. "I wouldn't want you to take this even to Minneapolis. Now, let's see."

He led me to a storage room, asking my dimensions on the way, then picked out a full uniform, complete from the skin out. Back at the locker, he said, "Here's a cap. Want another for your father?"

"That'd be great," I said.

"And your brother? Do you have a brother?"

"He'd love one," I said.

So Fitzie gave me three caps.

"Now about shoes?" he asked. "You shouldn't go out there in those things. What size do you wear?"

When I told him, he went off and came back with two brand-new pairs of shoes. "Keep 'em both," he said. "You'll need 'em in Minneapolis. How are you fixed for bats?"

"I thought I'd borrow somebody's here," I said.

"Ought to have your own," Fitzie said. "What weight do you use?"

He was back with two bats. "These all right?"

I picked one up, swung it a couple of times, and nodded. Fitzie grinned and said, "Take them to Minneapolis too. One more thing—"

He went off again and came back with a box of baseballs. "Here's a dozen autographed balls," he said. "Give 'em to your friends."

I was still getting ready when John Murphy, the farm director, came down. "I heard you were here," he said. "Have you got everything you need?"

"Fitzie's taking good care of me," I said.

"Fine. Now after the workout there are a few people I'd like you to meet. Then we'll go upstairs and see Mr. Yawkey. I'll see you outside."

When I was all suited up, Fitzie said, "Go on out and knock 'em dead. Only don't try to kill the ball. They know what you can do. They just want to look at you. Go down the steps and through the runway."

When I reached the field, Murphy introduced me to Rudy York, the batting coach, and one or two others, then told York to let me hit. By then I had forgotten my early nervousness and my experience with Orlando, and felt very much at home. And, once in the batting cage, I stood calmly at the plate, my eyes on the pitcher and everything blotted out of my thoughts but the baseball.

I hit it hard, far, and often that day. As usual, the name of the pitcher slips my mind, but I do remember hitting a couple into the bullpen in right, and one into the bleachers in right center, and several off the wall in left and left center. When they told me to get my glove and work out in the field, I felt wonderful. And when I got back to the clubhouse I finally met Ted Williams.

Nobody had to introduce us. He came over from his corner of the room, held out his hand, and said, "I'm Ted Williams."

"My name's Carl Yastrzemski."

"I know—I know all about you," he said. "Look, kid, don't ever—y'understand me?"—he raised his voice "—don't *ever* let anyone monkey with your swing."

Then he turned around and strode back across the room. It was the only time he spoke to me in the three days I stayed around Boston.

After I got back into street clothes, Murphy took me to meet Billy Jurges, then the manager. Short, gray-haired, soft-spoken, he shook hands, gave me a few words of encouragement, and told me he hoped to see me in Boston permanently. Then Murphy and I went upstairs to meet Tom Yawkey.

Perhaps because I had time to think on the way up, I was nearly as nervous as I had been before leaving the hotel for the ball park that morning. To me, Yawkey was as much a hero as Williams. He had waited so patiently so long for another Red Sox pennant—even then, they hadn't won one in thirteen years —yet never complained and continued to be as generous as ever to his ballplayers. This man was, and indeed still is, one of baseball's great figures, and the prospect of meeting him was a thrill.

Stocky, with china-blue eyes and close-cropped hair, then more black than gray, he had the ability to put anyone at ease. He smiled broadly as he held out his hand, looked me up and down, and said, "Pleasure to meet you, Carl. I watched you out there. You sure have a beautiful swing. You'll be up here before you know it."

He asked about my family and background, congratulated me on my great season at Raleigh, and told me he looked forward to seeing me in a Red Sox uniform in a year or two.

Some of the sports writers didn't want to wait that long. They demanded that I start playing in Boston immediately, pointing out that the ball club wasn't going anywhere and had no regular second baseman anyhow. Pete Runnels, in the line-up for his hitting, played there as much as anyone, and behind him was Pumpsie Green. The writers wanted to see me there for the rest of the season, but the Red Sox had already decided to send me to Minneapolis. Besides, Jurges pointed out that I might lose more than I'd gain by staying. "The pitchers are sharp now," he said. "The kid has never seen anything better than Class B pitching, and I'm afraid he'll get discouraged. We only have about twenty-five games to go. It would take him that long to get used to it up here."

I arrived at Minneapolis at four o'clock on the afternoon of September 15 and, to my surprise, was met at the airport and taken directly to the ball park. There Gene Mauch, the Millers' brilliant young manager—he hadn't yet turned thirty-four—asked me if I was ready and if I minded going right into the line-up in a playoff game against Omaha that night. He couldn't have given me a more welcome greeting. I told him getting right into the line-up was the one thing I wanted to do most.

"Just have to check your eligibility for this series," Mauch said. "But you take batting practice, and we'll know by the time you're through."

I didn't know until twenty minutes before the game if I was

going to play or not, then Gene told me I was okay. He hadn't seen Ed Doherty, the president of the American Association, but somebody in Doherty's office had given him permission to use me.

It was a seven-game series, all tied at two games apiece by the time I got there. We made it 3–2 when I got a single in the tenth inning off a pitcher named Frank Barnes and scored the winning run. Mauch was the first to congratulate me, but it was a false alarm. The Omaha club protested that I wasn't eligible, Doherty upheld the protest, and the game had to be played over.

While I watched from the bench, Minneapolis won a double-header to clinch the series the next day, sending us into the finals against Fort Worth. I couldn't play until September 20, since I was replacing a man who went into the Army on September 18 and two games in a row were rained out. At Fort Worth I finally got into a game that counted, collected three hits in four times up, scored three runs, drove in two more, and helped win a 9–6 ball game. I had a real good series, getting at least one hit in every game I played, and we beat Fort Worth to land in the Junior World Series against Havana, the International League champions.

It was, I'm sure, the daffiest post-season series in the history of organized baseball. The first three games were supposed to be in Minneapolis, but it snowed the day before the first game, and the temperature when we opened was 30 degrees. They had maybe twenty-five hundred out that day, and the next, with the weather no warmer, there were barely a thousand people in the stands. Everyone threw in the towel, and by mutual agreement we all went to Havana to finish the series.

My first impression of Havana was sheer fright at the driving, all of which seemed to be done with horns. The road from the airport to the hotel was an obstacle course of cars, trucks, and buses handled by maniacs who didn't care where they were going but how fast. Every minute on that highway was an adventure, with the odds against anybody's getting anywhere alive. When we reached the Havana Hilton we were all nervous wrecks.

We had an old ball club, made up mostly of veterans who were on their way down, and Mauch didn't want me, the youngest guy on the team, fraternizing with any of them. He roomed me with Lu Clinton, the only one anywhere near me in age; he was a couple of years older than I. It was hot, and we stripped down to our shorts and ordered dinner sent up to our room, a convenience Mauch had already arranged for everybody.

While we were waiting to eat Clinton said, "Yaz, you got a pretty good bonus, didn't you?"

When I nodded, he said, "Then how come you wear such lousy clothes?"

"What's the matter with my clothes?" I asked.

"Look," he said, picking up an old pair of chinos. "You walked into the hotel in these things."

"They were all right in Raleigh."

"You're in Triple A now," Clinton said. "You might be in the big leagues by next year. You shouldn't go around in pants like this. And look at this beat-up old shirt. How can a $100,000 bonus kid wear junk like this? And this? And this?"

As he talked, he gathered up the only two pairs of pants and the only three shirts I had with me, as well as my underwear and socks, went to the window, and threw them all out. Then he got my moth-eaten sports jacket, which I had been wearing since I first entered Notre Dame, and threw that out. My scuffed shoes went next. Finally he picked up my frayed old wallet, took out the money and the papers, and tossed that out. All the junk landed on a low roof nineteen floors down, and I sadly watched it bounce around.

With nothing left but the shorts and socks I wore, I said, "What do I do now?"

Clinton pointed to the money from the wallet.

"How much?"

"Maybe a thousand," I said.

"For fifty bucks you can get a whole new wardrobe down here," he said. "First thing in the morning we'll go shopping."

"In what?" I said.

"I'll lend you something," he said.

At least those old clothes of mine didn't go to waste. When we got up the next morning they were gone. And by eleven o'clock, with Clinton's help, I had the newest wardrobe in Havana.

There was a big parade for us that afternoon, climaxed by a two-hour speech by Fidel Castro, and late in the day we had an armed escort to Gran Stadium. The whole of Havana looked like an armed camp, with fuzzy-faced kids and bearded men carrying carbines and submachine guns all over the place. None of us was very comfortable, but Gene Mauch kept telling us not to worry. He knew that Fidel wouldn't let anything bad happen to us. Castro, who had just taken over Cuba the previous January, was still more hero than villain in the eyes of the free world, and an ardent baseball fan besides. He lived at our hotel and told Mauch he'd be at all the games.

On the way to the ball park we were uncomfortable, but after we got there we were scared to death. The place was so mobbed that the field was roped off to allow crowds to stand along the foul lines. There were armed guards around us all the time. They escorted us as a group to the locker room, and individually when we came out, then stayed in the dugouts all through the game. The guy who wrote that it was the first series with more submachine guns than bats didn't exaggerate. There were submachine guns all over the ball park, and bats only on the field. Trigger-happy kids wandered around with their guns at the ready, and every once in a while one went off.

Batting practice was canceled when the soldiers started stealing the balls out of Joe Mooney's bag. Joe, the Millers' equipment man, had gone out to the field with about three dozen of them, and we were supposed to follow. But the minute we arrived in the dugout, a few of those young armed guards reached right into his bag. He picked it up and fled back to the locker room, but not before losing half the balls.

A guy came in and said, "Hang on to everything you own. Don't put your glove or anything else down on the bench unless you want to lose it. Watch out that nobody takes your cap.

And keep your eye on your shoes. You never know when some guy might try to grab them right off your feet."

I didn't know whether the guards who took us from the locker room to the dugout were friends or enemies. They hustled us out of one place into another so fast that I was on the bench before I knew it. The game was supposed to start at eight-thirty, but eight-thirty came and went and there wasn't even a sign of the umpires.

"They're waiting for Fidel," somebody said. "Can't start until he gets here."

Fidel didn't show up for an hour. Even though we couldn't have batting practice, Mauch wanted us to warm up, but first he had to find someone who could keep the soldiers from stealing our baseballs. When the guy who seemed to be in charge of the guard promised we'd be left alone, Mauch told us to go out and get loose. We lost a few balls but managed to save most of them.

At about nine-thirty a helicopter started coming down, and the crowd chanted, "Fidel, Fidel, Fidel," while the trigger-happy kids shot off their guns and we cringed in the dugout. The helicopter landed at second base, and Castro stepped out, grinning and waving and smoking a cigar which you could hardly see in the night lights because his black beard was in the way. He went right to a seat behind home plate, the umpires came out, Mauch and Manager Preston Gomez of the Havana Club handed them the line-ups, and we were finally ready to go.

The series went the full seven games, and we lost it by blowing a two-run lead in the eighth and ninth innings of the last one. I suppose it was just as well. If we had won, we probably wouldn't have got out of there alive. I did fairly well—hit around .310 and had a couple of homers. One landed about 450 feet from the plate in dead center field. Castro, who sat behind the plate only for the first game, moved around for the other games and happened to be sitting right near where the ball landed. After the game he came into the locker room, shook hands with me, and said, "Grand home run," which I guess was about all the English he knew.

That night Mauch threw a big party for us at the Hilton. He had a couple of suites on the twenty-third floor and let everyone do as he pleased. Clinton and I stuck pretty much together, while the older guys raised all the hell. Somewhere around four in the morning Mauch gave us the money to buy enough spareribs for the whole party in a joint across the street, and Lu and I went down for them. We brought back pounds and pounds, which were gone in half an hour. After Mauch went to bed, somebody threw a glass out the window, and it landed right in the middle of the swimming pool, twenty-three floors below. That started a glass-throwing contest which lasted until the hotel manager came up with a couple of cops who threatened to take us all to the pokey. They had to get Mauch up to straighten out the mess. He told us to quit throwing glasses into the pool and went back to bed.

By then it was seven in the morning and the commuter traffic was getting heavy. "Oh, well," somebody said, "nobody told us we couldn't throw glasses at the cars." So while Clinton and I watched in morbid fascination, the boys began popping glasses on the pavement while scared Cubans got out of their cars to see who was shooting at them. That brought the cops right back, and again they wanted to arrest all of us.

Mauch finally came in and when he found out what was going on he said, "Don't take anybody anywhere until I call Fidel."

The mention of Fidel stopped everyone. Castro had told Mauch to call him any time we needed him, and Mauch knew we'd never need him more than now. He had a time getting through, but finally reached Castro, who came right down. Fidel told the cops to get out, then, through his interpreter, said, "Don't throw any more glasses." He and Mauch jabbered for a minute, then Gene said, "Okay. Everybody to his room. Pack up. We're leaving in twenty minutes."

Castro gave us an armed escort to the airport, but we didn't know whether those guys were friends or enemies either. After we arrived, a couple of the soldiers got a little rough while the guy in charge began raising a fuss with Mauch about something.

Gene finally turned and said, "Don't anybody move. I've got to call Fidel again."

Fidel's name helped a little, I guess. At least nobody took a shot at us. But we were surrounded by our escort, and none of us was allowed to go anywhere but the men's room for the next four hours. Then Gene got back, yelled, "Okay, everybody on the plane," and we couldn't get out of there fast enough.

Thanks to Mauch I collected a full losers' share of the series money, about $600. Lu Clinton told me afterward that the boys had voted me a half-share, but Mauch said, "He gets a full share. We wouldn't have been in the series without him."

The last thing Mauch told me after we got home was, "You've got it, kid. Stay in shape and show 'em next spring that you belong up there."

Although spring training at Scottsdale in 1960 was a social flop because only the Malzones paid any attention to us, it appeared to be a professional triumph for me. I played in something like ten straight games, hitting the ball hard and consistently, not making any errors, pivoting well on double plays, and leading the team in batting. With the Red Sox a dying ball club—Ted Williams was in his last year, and the only other real hitter they had was Pete Runnels—I was getting plenty of publicity, and pretty soon I figured Manager Billy Jurges would have to shift Runnels from second base to first to make room for me.

My folks came out from Bridgehampton, and while they were there I had a great day against the San Francisco Giants, whom we beat in an exhibition game, 6–5. I drove in four of our six runs with a homer and a double, pivoted on two double plays, and handled about six chances without an error. When I got home that night I told Carol and Dad, "I'm going to make this ball club."

"Well, don't get your hopes up too high," Dad said. "They may have other plans for you."

He must have known something because a day or two later one of the writers told me he heard I was going back to the Millers. The next day Jurges said, "You're one of the best youngsters I've ever seen, and we don't want you sitting on the bench half the time. We're sending you to Minneapolis, where you can play every day."

I was furious—mad at Jurges, mad at Bucky Harris, the general manager, mad at the other Red Sox ballplayers for giving me the cold shoulder, mad at the world. Carol and Dad calmed me down, and I flew to Deland, Florida, where the Minneapolis club trained. On the way I realized that at least one of my blessings would be a reunion with Gene Mauch, and by the time I arrived in Deland I didn't feel so bad.

The first thing Mauch said was, "You did all right out there. How do you feel about playing for me again?"

"I like playing for you," I said. "I just didn't like being sent down."

"Never saw a guy who did," Gene said. "Maybe they should have kept you."

He peered at me, then said casually, "We're shifting you to left field."

Ted Williams' job, I thought. *So that's why they sent me down.*

"Big shoes," I said.

"You can fill 'em," Mauch said. "Take tomorrow off, and we'll go to work the next day."

I spent a lot of time talking baseball with Mauch in the next ten days. He was tough, but very fair, a guy who asked nothing from you but your best, which any manager is entitled to. Over and over, he worked on my confidence, building me up so that I wouldn't go back to Boston fearful that the job he was grooming me for would be more than I could handle.

"You're no Ted Williams yet," he used to say. "But some day you can be better than he is. In your own way you'll be as good a hitter, and you're already a better fielder."

He hit fungoes to me by the hour, getting me used to taking long flies. I had hated the outfield in semi-pro ball, where the fences were either way out or nonexistent, but there was no such problem in organized ball. Fences were a reasonable distance away, wherever you played, and the only problem was learning the peculiarities of individual ball parks. Mauch, who had once played for the Red Sox, described the left-field fence at Fenway Park in detail, and was the first to tell me of the problems I would have there.

He called me "Irish" because I went to Notre Dame, and he treated me more like a kid brother than like a ballplayer working for him. He took me to breakfast a few times, and even got me a deal on a new car and arranged for it to be shipped to Minneapolis. He changed my whole attitude. I lost my bitterness and looked forward to the season.

Three days before we broke camp, Mauch came over to me, held out his hand, and said, "Good luck, Irish. Remember what I told you. You've got it and you'll make it big. I'd like to have had you for another year, but I'm going to manage the Phillies."

I couldn't have felt worse if somebody had punched me in the stomach. Here was a guy who had done everything for me in the short time I knew him, a guy for whom I was ready to work like a dog, a guy I hoped might some day manage the Red Sox, and suddenly he was gone.

Later in the day Charlie Schilling, my roommate, said, "I hope Pop takes his place."

"Pop" was Eddie Popowski, a wonderful little man from New Jersey whom I had met the year before at the Red Sox rookie camp in Ocala, Florida, where I first met Schilling. Pop was everybody's friend. He could make the sun shine in a rainstorm for a kid who was down. He had managed Schilling the year before at Alpine in the Sophomore League, and, in common with everyone else who knew him, Charlie was crazy about him.

Pop did get the job and joined us the next day. And, thanks to him, I had my most enjoyable season up to 1967, when the Red Sox won the pennant. The thing that made Pop was his eternal optimism. He knew something kids don't know—that there's always tomorrow if you had a bad day today. When he said, "Don't worry, you'll be all right," he wasn't being a cheer-leader. He was telling you he had confidence in you, and that gave you confidence.

He and Schilling had adjoining rooms at the Hotel Maryland in Minneapolis. They ate breakfast together every morning that year, both at home and on the road, where I joined them. Pop talked nothing but baseball, for his whole life was wrapped up in the game. Too small to be a big-leaguer—he stood less than 5 feet, 5 inches—he made up in spiritual stature what he lacked in physical stature. Just being with him gave us a lift.

He couldn't solve every problem, and he didn't try. When I went into a terrible slump early in the season, I asked him if he minded my calling my dad for help.

"If you think your dad can help you, go ahead," Pop said.

Mom and Dad came straight through from Bridgehampton to Minneapolis, one sleeping while the other drove, and went right to the ball park without even checking into the hotel. Then, with Pop pitching to me, Dad watched me hit for an hour and a half.

"You're crouching too much," he finally said. "Straighten up a little. And you're not holding your bat at quite the proper angle." That night I got three hits, and Pop said, "Next time you need him, don't even ask me."

I blew my stack in July when the Red Sox called up Lu Clinton instead of me after Gary Geiger, one of their regular outfielders, suffered a lung collapse. I was hitting over .300, and Lu was around .260. We were at the airport getting ready to leave Indianapolis when we got the news, and I was so upset I walked up to the counter, threw down my ticket to Charleston, West Virginia, and said, "Give me a ticket for Minneapolis."

Pop, standing beside me, just looked up and quietly said, "What are you going to Minneapolis for?"

"I'm going to pick up Carol and take her to Long Island," I said. "I've had it in this organization. They can trade me to somebody else."

"Maybe they won't trade you," Pop said. "What will you do then?"

"Wait until they do trade me," I said.

"But what if they don't?" he said.

I began stammering around, and Pop said, "You're mad because they sent you down last spring, not because they took Clinton now instead of you. What do you think they'd do with you up there, bench Ted Williams to make room for you?"

"Well, I don't like the way they're treating me," I said.

"You want to play center field?" Pop said. "Or right field? Or sit on the bench?"

"They didn't have to send me down in the first place," I said.

"They thought you were big enough to take Williams' place," Pop said. "You think maybe they made a mistake?"

The flight to Charleston was called. Pop said, "Don't forget your ticket," and I picked it up off the counter and followed him out to the plane.

I finished the season in a blaze of glory, hitting safely in the last 37 games in a row. I was just a couple of hits under .500 from August 1 until September 8, when the season ended. It gave me a .339 average, five points behind Larry Osborne of Denver, who won the batting title, but I was disappointed that I hit only seven home runs. Still, I won the league's Most Valuable Player award and really didn't have any complaints.

Instead of calling me up to sit on the bench, the Red Sox gave me the rest of the year off. I went back to Notre Dame with nothing on my mind except my studies, the coming birth of Maryann, our first child, and the prospect of replacing Ted Williams in left field for the Red Sox.

CHAPTER 7

That Man Ted Williams

When I first went to spring training with the Red Sox in 1960 I was too afraid of Ted Williams to talk much to him. All I knew about him was what I read in the papers—that he was insulting, contemptuous, and profane, and that, no matter who was around, he said what he pleased. Later, when I got to know him, I found him a marvelous guy, for he was always great to me, but in those days he scared me half to death. He talked in such a loud voice that you could hear him at the rodeo next door to our ball field, and some of the things he said would curl your hair. His favorite expression when a guy didn't understand what he was trying to teach was, "You stupid jerk," only he didn't say "jerk." I wasn't about to have him call me that in front of a whole lot of people.

Yet I desperately wanted to talk to him, to ask him what I was doing wrong, to get him to show me how I could improve. But I was just a twenty-year-old kid and he was Ted Williams, and I didn't think it was my place to go to him. I didn't learn until later that he never approached anyone with unsolicited advice. He felt the guy who needed help would go to him, but I didn't dare. Except for a handshake when we first met at Scottsdale, we had practically no direct contact. The best I could do was try to learn something by overhearing what he told others.

And when Williams talked about hitting, believe me, everybody listened. They can talk about Babe Ruth and Ty Cobb and Rogers Hornsby and Lou Gehrig and Joe DiMaggio and Stan Musial and all the rest, but I'm sure not one of them could hold cards and spades to Williams in his sheer knowledge of hitting, of how to read pitchers, of what to expect and why to expect it, of how to cover every fraction of an inch of the strike zone, of when to swing for homers and when to settle for something less, of how to pull out of slumps, and of every other conceivable facet of the art of hitting a baseball. He studied hitting the way a broker studies the stock market, and could spot at a glance mistakes that others couldn't see in a week.

His knowledge of pitching and pitchers was just as thorough. I'm told that whenever the opposing team had a new pitcher, Williams couldn't wait to watch him work. As with hitters, he didn't just look at pitchers, he *studied* them. Pitchers are the natural enemies of hitters, and Williams always wanted to know exactly what a pitcher had, how he used what he had, what his pitching patterns were, and everything else about him. Even during my time at Scottsdale, Williams would go into lengthy discussions about a pitcher, pointing out his strengths and his weaknesses and how and when he could be most easily hit.

That 1960 season was Williams' last as an active player. When I returned to Scottsdale in 1961 as his successor in left field, he came out as special batting instructor. Maybe because he knew I was being groomed to take his place, he watched me closely. The first day he was there, he stood behind the batting cage, yelling, "You look great, Yaz, you're doing fine," and all that sort of thing. I didn't ask him anything specific until one day I realized pitchers were jamming me, throwing the ball in tight to me so I couldn't get the fat of the bat on it. Not knowing what to do, I went over to Williams and said, "Ted, can I talk to you a little about hitting?"

"Sure," he said. "Let's go down to the cage and work with Iron Mike." Iron Mike is our pitching machine.

On the way to the cage he talked what sounded at first like Greek to me. "You've got to remember four things, Yaz," he said. Then, raising his voice: "Four things, y'understand?"

Before I could ask what four things, he said, "Number one, close your stance and back away from the plate and stand deep in the batter's box. That'll let you hit the ball here at this angle" —pointing to an imaginary plate and an imaginary angle— "instead of hitting the ball out in front. The reason is you can make more mistakes and still hit the ball. Okay? To hit the ball perfectly you have to pull it, you have to hit everything out here" —pointing—"and you only hit that part of the bat. You have to be out front. When you're out front you only have that much of the bat to work with. Four inches. That's to hit the ball perfectly, to pull. But when you're in trouble you have to hit the ball behind you a little bit. That way, you can make a mistake and maybe get away with it because you've got six inches to play with. Okay?"

He talked fast and loud, and I didn't have the foggiest notion of what he meant. All I knew was that I used a closed stance anyhow, and I didn't see how I could close it any more.

"Number two," Williams said. "Watch the ball." He raised his voice. "*Watch the ball.* Don't ever take your eyes off it. *Ever.* Okay?"

"Right," I said. That one I could understand.

"Number three, hit the ball back through the middle. Hit everything—*everything*—back at the pitcher. Forget about pulling. That comes later. *Don't pull.* Y'understand? Through the middle. Okay?"

"Right," I said.

"Number four," Williams said. "Be quick with your hands and watch for your pitch. Be quick—quick." Up came the voice again. "And know your pitch. *Know your pitch.* And be quick. Okay?"

"Right," I said, only it wasn't quite right. I couldn't figure out exactly what he meant by knowing my pitch. I liked some pitches better than others, but it couldn't have been that simple. He had something else in mind. And that closed stance business also bothered me. I wanted to ask Williams about that too, but I didn't dare. A lot of people had followed us down to Iron Mike, and I didn't want him calling me a stupid jerk in front of them.

"Go on in the cage and try now," Williams said.

As I swung, Williams kept yelling little tips. "Back away from the plate. . . . Back away. . . . Two strikes, choke the bat. . . . You're trying to pull. . . . Hit the ball back through the middle. . . . Aim it at the pitcher. . . . That's's it . . . good . . . good . . . back away . . . back away . . . watch the ball . . . be quick . . . quick . . . quick. . . ."

I worked for an hour. Then, before leaving, Williams said, "Four things, Yaz, remember. Number one, close your stance and back away. Number two, watch the ball. Number three, hit the ball through the middle. Number four, be quick."

He said it a couple more times, and from then on, every time I ran into him, he said one or all of them. The afternoon of our first session he passed me on the way to the shower and said, "Be quick, be quick." That night I saw him getting out of a car, and he yelled, "Watch the ball." In the clubhouse the next day he brushed by me on the way to his locker, saying, "Four things. Say them over and over. Make them part of you. Close your stance and back away. Watch the ball. Hit the ball through the middle. Be quick."

I hit well for a while, then ran into trouble and went to Williams again. He made me recite his four rules, then said, "Okay, let's watch you swing." I stood at the plate, and Williams, from behind the screen, yelled, "You're trying to pull. Hit it through the middle."

Later he quizzed me. "Why do you go into a slump?" he said.

"Because I'm trying to pull the ball," I said.

"Why is it harder to pull than to hit it down the middle?"

"Because you have to hit it perfectly to pull, but you can make a mistake and still hit it down the middle or to the wrong field."

"What about your hands?"

"Quick."

"Your eyes?"

"On the ball," I said.

"Your stance?"

"Closed.

"And where do you stand?"

"Away," I said.

We went through this routine over and over, a teacher and a pupil repeating by rote all the rules of the game. Sometimes I got sick of it, but Williams never did. He repeated and repeated and repeated, and made me repeat after him.

"You go to sleep with it in your head," he said. "You wake up with it in your head. After a while it's as natural as breathing."

When I did well he stood behind the cage, yelling encouragement, repeating his rules, and when I was through he said, "Great. You're getting it." Then he said them again, and I said, "Yes, Ted. . . . Right, Ted. . . . Okay, Ted. . . . I get it, Ted."

When I got impatient, I said, "I'm all straightened out, Ted. I've got it. I'm thinking exactly what you want me to think." Then Williams said, "I don't have to tell you anything. You look great, just great."

And he was right—for a few days. But then another dip would come, and I'd have to go back to him. I used to go home and tell Carol, "It's the most amazing thing. I get into trouble and go to Williams and he tells me the same thing all the time and that gets me out of the trouble. Why can't I do these things for myself?"

Carol didn't know and didn't try to explain it. And when I look back on it now, I can't explain it either. All I know is that the man was a marvel at getting things unraveled when they were all snagged up. And everything always boiled down to his four basic rules.

I worried about not understanding the fine points of those rules, and didn't get them cleared up in my mind all that year. It took a couple of seasons before I really saw what he had been driving at when he talked about my closed stance and knowing my pitch. He hadn't really meant for me to close my stance any more, because it already was closed. The important thing was to back away from the plate, to stand deeper in the box. And when he talked of my knowing my pitch, it wasn't to hit the pitch I liked best, but the one I expected a specific pitcher to throw.

"You can't afford to have a favorite pitch," he once said. "You have to know your pitcher and what he's most likely to give you. After you decide that, you look for it and are prepared to hit it."

Sometimes he watched me a minute at the plate and said, "You worry too much. You're trying to get things down too fine. You're a perfectionist."

After I came out of the cage he made me recite the four rules again, then talked about my being a perfectionist. Once I said, "What's wrong with being a perfectionist? Aren't you one?"

"Sure I am," he said. "And you will be after a few years. But don't try to run before you can walk. Learn the fundamentals, and the fine points will come. You worry too much. You think too much."

Always he stressed the importance of knowing pitchers. "Don't ever let a pitcher get you out twice on the same pitch," he said. "Learn what he gets you out on and be prepared for it. And know his best pitch, because you'll see it. A good hitter should be able to anticipate the pitch that's coming seventy-five to eighty per cent of the time. You watch and you learn and you remember."

If I was a little slow with my hands, he picked up a bat, moved into the cage, and started hitting the ball with that marvelous swing of his. The more I watched, the more I realized his power came from his wrists, not his arms or his body. A quick flick of those wrists and the ball sailed 400 feet out into right field, a perfectly pulled shot.

How can I replace this guy? I thought. *How can anyone? There'll never be another hitter like him.*

The last time I saw him in Arizona before he took off for his home in the Florida Keys, he shook hands and boomed, "Don't forget, don't forget. Close the stance and back away deep in the box. Watch the ball. *Watch the ball.* Hit the ball through the middle. Look for your pitch and be quick—*be quick.*"

When the ball club reached Boston for the season's opener, I was puzzled to read stories in the newspapers that the Red Sox were trying to get me to pull the ball more. Actually, this was just the opposite of what Williams had been telling me all spring. He didn't want me to pull. I weighed only about 165 pounds at the time, and maybe Williams felt I wasn't big enough, hadn't filled out enough yet, to pull effectively. In any event, he wanted me to get those fundamentals down pat first. He had said the pulling would come later, and, as it developed, that was exactly what happened.

I don't know where those stories about the Red Sox worrying over my failure to pull came from. Maybe they were telling the writers they were worried, but they never told me. All Mike Higgins, the manager, ever said was, "Don't worry. No matter what happens you're my left fielder." At the beginning of the season it wasn't necessary for him to say any more. To be told by the boss that I wouldn't lose my job even if I didn't hit well starting out was all the assurance I needed.

There was a lot of talk around town about the pressure I faced trying to replace a man who had been Boston's baseball idol since before I was born, but I had been only vaguely aware of that pressure during the winter and really not a bit aware of it in the spring. Actually, there was pressure enough simply trying to make it in the big leagues, whether I was replacing Ted Williams or a nonentity. That I happened to be playing Williams' old position didn't make the pressure any worse.

I got away to a horrible start. Big-league pitching is altogether different from Triple A, which technically is only one step down the ladder but actually is in another world. The major-leaguers know how to pitch. There are more top-ranking pitchers in the majors. Down in the American Association you might face a good pitcher once every three or four days. In the big leagues you faced first-class pitching all the time. There was no relief, no chance to relax, no soft spot, and I was having nothing but trouble.

Day after day, and over and over, I repeated Ted Williams' four fundamental rules to myself. I knew them and could recite them by heart, but now I saw I didn't yet understand them well enough to apply them to myself. There was something radically wrong. Except for occasional short periods, I didn't feel comfortable at the plate, and when I didn't feel comfortable I rarely hit the ball well.

Higgins knew something was wrong, but I think he figured it was psychological, because whenever we met he just patted me on the back and told me to stay in there swinging. "You have a good swing," he said. "You'll be all right. Just have patience." I was grateful for his assurance, but now I needed concrete help and had no idea where to turn for it.

As far as I could tell, I was doing everything just as I always had. I batted from a crouch, as I do now, with my stance closed (part of the first rule of Ted Williams), I tried to watch the ball (the second rule of Ted Williams), I tried to hit it through the middle (the third rule of Ted Williams), and I tried to be quick (part of the fourth rule of Ted Williams). I still hadn't been able to apply the rest of the fourth rule—picking my pitch and waiting for it—because I still didn't thoroughly understand it.

Whatever the reason, the pitchers were jamming me to death. Word about any promising rookie gets around the league fast, and pretty soon every pitcher in the American League knew something about me. Despite Higgins' encouragement, which I welcomed and appreciated, I was very nervous and upset, because my batting average hovered around .210, and how long could I expect even the patient Higgins to put up with a .210 hitter in left field?

When I had a good day in Detroit late in June, I thought perhaps I was pulling out of the mess. I felt good in batting practice before the game, and got a couple of hits, including a long home run into the right-center-field stands. That night, Charlie Schilling, my pal and roomie, told me he thought I'd be all right, that I had looked better at the plate than I had all season. Schilling, outhitting me by about 70 points, had done something I couldn't do—forced Pete Runnels off second base. Runnels was now playing first, with Charlie the regular second baseman.

"Tomorrow we get Lary," I said.

"When you're hitting, it doesn't matter who you get," Schilling said.

Frank Lary, one of the best right-handers in baseball, was having his greatest season; he ended up winning 23 games for the Tigers that year. The one time I had faced him I did fairly well, and this time I hoped to do better. During batting practice I felt good, and I went into the game thinking I was about to knock Lary and the Tigers dead.

My first time up the count went to 1 ball and 1 strike; then Lary jammed me with a good hard inside pitch and splintered my bat. I hit a little dribbler down to second for an easy out, and when I got back to the dugout I thought, *That was a slider. Ted says look for the pitches he gets you on. Okay, I'll look for the slider.*

I opened my stance a little next time up, ready to hit the first slider Lary threw. But his first pitch was a sinker, a called strike on the outside corner. *Now for the slider,* I thought. I waited and watched, and Lary threw me another sinker right to the same spot. I let it go by for a second called strike and dug in for the slider I was sure would come next. Only it wasn't the slider. He threw me a third sinker on the outside corner, I let it go by for a strike, and I was out of there without lifting my bat off my shoulder.

He won't get me again, I thought. *I'm a fast-ball hitter. I'll go up there looking for that sinker next time, and I'll cream the ball.* That was what Williams taught: look for the pitch he got you on the last time. Up I went for the third time, and Lary jammed me three times in a row with sliders. I went out swinging, and when my fourth time came I didn't know what to look for. I forgot everything Williams told me, forgot everything I had known before, forgot that I had hit .377 at Raleigh and .339 at Minneapolis, and thought only that I had been lucky to get this far and that now I was through. I don't even remember what Lary threw that time, only that I hit an inside pitch on the handle and went out on a little infield roller.

Oh for four—two strikeouts, one when I got caught looking, and two infield outs in four trips to the plate. On the plane back to Boston that night I nearly broke down and cried. When Charlie tried to cheer me up, I almost bit his head off.

"Don't let it get you, Carl," he said. "You'll pull out of it."

"You can talk," I snapped. "You're hitting .275. But look at me, the hotshot kid who's supposed to be the new Ted Williams. I'm down around .200, and I'll be under it in a couple of days."

Fitzie couldn't help either. He came over to me while we were still flying, patted me on the back, and told me not to worry.

"That's what everybody says—don't worry, don't worry," I said. "How can I not worry?" Then I suddenly got an idea. "Do you think Mr. Yawkey might help?"

"He'll be glad to," Fitzie said.

"Will he talk to me?" I said.

"Sure he will."

"I've got to see him," I said. "I'll go in tomorrow."

We were off the next day, but I called Mr. Yawkey and made a date to see him at the ball park.

"You've given me all this money and I'm letting you down," I said. "I can't go on like this."

"You're young and you're a natural," he said. "You'll come around. I know you will."

"But I need help now," I said. "I'm confused. I'm upset. I'm stuck. I don't know what to do or where to turn. I wish Ted were here."

He looked at me, his blue eyes bright. "You want Ted?" he said. Then: "You know, I think that's the answer." He picked up the phone and told the operator to get Ted Williams. Ten minutes later she called back, said something, and Yawkey said, "I don't care if he's out in the middle of the ocean. They must have a radio aboard. Get hold of him somehow."

He turned to me and said, "Be dressed and ready to hit at ten in the morning."

"You think Ted will be here then?" I said.

"He'll be here."

On the dot of ten the next morning I went through the runway from the Red Sox clubhouse to the dugout, and the first guy I saw when I stepped out on the field was Ted Williams. In slacks and a white shirt, he was leaning against the rail beside the dugout, talking to Tom Yawkey. Joe Coleman, a former big-league pitcher who threw a lot of batting practice for us, was warming up out on the mound. Sal Maglie, our pitching coach, and Rudy York, the batting coach, were around, and several kids were on the field ready to shag.

"Hello, Yaz," Williams said in that big booming voice, "how are you? And what the hell's the matter? Come on, come on"— he led the way to the dugout—"let's sit down and talk before you go out to hit. What's the problem?"

"I'm all mixed up," I said. "I keep going over those four rules—"

"Wait a minute, wait a minute," Williams said. "Let's start from the beginning. I saw you here when you came up from Raleigh just after you hit .377. You swinging the same way now?"

"I think so," I said.

"Standing the same way? Holding your hands the same way? Doing everything the same way?"

I nodded.

"Are you sure? Are you sure?" Williams asked. "I'll tell you how you hit." And he told me how I was standing, where my hips were, and my arms and my shoulders and my hands. He described every move I made at the plate and kept asking, "You still doing this? You still doing that?"

Then he said, "Okay. How about at spring training? You were doing everything right then. Do you remember exactly what you did?"

As we talked, Williams drew me out. "What do you need?" he said. "What do you want to know? Ask me. Don't be afraid."

"Well, for one thing," I said, "I never understood why you insisted on my closing my stance when I used about as closed a stance as I could already."

"Because I thought it would help you," he said. "I'll watch you hit, and we'll see. How about your crouch? Have you changed that any?"

"Not that I know of," I said.

"Well, we'll see. You've been standing deep in the box? Watching the ball? Hitting the ball through the middle? Being quick with your hands and looking for your pitch?"

I told him what happened with Lary, and he grinned. "Pitchers will do that—smart pitchers. You can't dope them out every time. If you could, you'd bat 1.000. Guy hits .333 today he's doing well, but that means he's getting fooled twice out of every three times up. Well"—he stood up—"let's see you hit."

I went to the plate, and Coleman began pitching to me while Williams watched from behind the batting cage. After I took a couple of swings, Williams roared, "Wait a minute, wait a minute."

He came around, stood next to me, and said, "Why the big crouch? You're down too low. Straighten up—not much, just a little." And, as I straightened: "Okay, okay, now you can get some use out of your knees so you can fluctuate your stance. Okay." He moved back behind the cage, and Coleman started pitching to me again.

I swung a few more times, and Williams yelled to Coleman, "Jam him, Joe, jam him." I moved deeper into the box, and

Williams said, "That's right, Yaz. Now just take your natural swing. Hit it down the middle, down the middle." More swings, then: "Open up a little, Yaz. Try that—okay."

On and on went the lesson, with Williams sometimes coming out from behind the cage, grabbing a bat, and standing at the plate in his slacks and his white shirt, swinging to demonstrate a point. I watched him hitting line drives and belts into the right-field bullpen with that fantastic swing and thought, *Why did he quit? He's better at his age than any guy mine.* Then he'd say, "See? Y'see, Yaz? Y'get it? Okay. Try it."

He made it look so easy, pulling the ball into the right-field seats apparently without any effort at all. When he hit I got behind the cage and marveled, for he looked like a golfer playing chip and putt, belting the ball these tremendous distances as though hitting a green with easy little nine-iron shots. I kept wanting to ask him how he did it, but never quite could. Even today, although I use my hands much better than I did then, I don't know how Williams did it, how a man of such height and strength could do so much with his hands and his wrists. I couldn't.

Sometimes after I had swung a few times Williams yelled, "Dammit, you're using too much body. Use your hands, your hands. And hit it through the middle." When I smacked three or four good ones in a row, he roared, "Great! That's the way to hit the ball. Hit it back to the pitcher. The pull will take care of itself. Okay. You're standing right. You're crouching right. You're striding right. Your hands are good."

The workout lasted an hour and a half, and I began feeling like a hitter again. Finally Williams said, "Okay, Yaz, you look good. But I'm not leaving until you're sure you're okay."

"I feel good," I said.

"Okay, okay. Now remember everything. And be quick— *quick.*"

He shook hands and went over to join Yawkey; then the two of them walked out through one of the lower grandstand entrances. I heard later that Yawkey had reached him by radio on a fishing boat out in the Atlantic. Williams went right into Miami and flew from there to Boston that morning. He came to the ball park, went back to the airport when the workout was over, returned to Florida, and was back on the boat before nightfall.

That night I hit two doubles, one off the wall in left center, the other to right center, and from then on I was in pretty good shape. I ended up at .266, which, while not great, wasn't bad, considering my start. And I felt comfortable at the plate all season. I went into an occasional mild slump but nothing as serious as before. The next year I hit .296 and the year after won the batting championship at .321. The only times I ever saw Williams were in the spring, when he appeared to help coach the hitters. Sometimes we talked, occasionally I asked him for help, but most of the time our meetings consisted of hellos and good-bys, with typical Williams reminders like, "Be quick, watch the ball, hit it down the middle," when we passed each other on the field or in the locker room.

One day in 1965, our last year of spring training at Scottsdale, Williams said, "Yaz, you're not hitting enough home runs. You've got the strength and the build and the maturity, and you know how to hit. But you've never had twenty homers in a season, and you should be averaging thirty or more."

"How do you make a home-run hitter out of a guy?" I said.

"I'll show you," he said. "Now, when you hit the ball perfectly you pull it because it will then go the farthest possible distance in your power alley, which is to right field. Up to now I've been telling you to hit the ball down the middle, down the middle. If you're in a slump, you still do that, because there's no better way to get out of one. But when you're going right, you should pull—pull purposely. Okay?"

"I pull every so often," I said.

"But not enough," he said. "And not purposely. When you pull, it's in the natural course of events. You're trying to hit the ball down the middle and you happen to get a clean shot at it and it goes out of the park in right field. But you shouldn't have to depend on that. You should be able to aim for those homers."

"How?"

"By turning your hips and your shoulders away from the pitcher. That lets you pivot better and gets more power into your swing."

I tried it a few times, but it didn't feel right. When I complained to Williams he said, "Work on it. You've got no business settling for sixteen, seventeen, eighteen home runs a season. With your ability and your strength, you ought to hit twice as many."

Now Williams was opening a whole new field for me, but also posing a whole new set of problems. Fearful that the new stance might set me back in other ways, I didn't take to it quickly, nor did it feel comfortable at all that spring. But Williams kept after me, worked with me, constantly reminded me that I hadn't reached my potential and never would until I began hitting more home runs. When we got home that year I was only half convinced.

But I did hit homers in clusters a couple of times during the season, and, even though I missed 35 games because of injuries, I piled up 20 home runs for the first time in my big-league career, while hitting .312. That made me feel pretty good, but when I saw Williams at Winter Haven, Florida, where we began spring training in 1966, he wasn't happy.

"For a guy like you twenty home runs is nothing," he said. "One thing—you lack confidence. If you don't think you'll hit a lot of homers, you won't."

"I'm afraid of getting out of my groove," I said.

"You're just strengthening your groove, not getting out of it," he said. "Close your hips. Show the pitcher more of your tail. You've got the power. Use it."

But I was less receptive then than the year before. Unable to get comfortable at the plate, I went back to my old style of hitting and had a lousy year. My .278 batting average was my worst since my rookie season, and I certainly didn't become the scourge of American League pitchers with my 16 home runs. That winter I had plenty of time to think, and one of several conclusions I came to was that Ted Williams, as always, was right. When I went south in the spring of 1967 I couldn't wait to talk to him.

"You say I can become a home-run hitter," I said. "I'm ready."

"Okay," he said. "You weren't ready before. That was the trouble. The secret of hitting homers is in your hips." And off he went into a long discourse on how to use my hips for leverage, how, if I turned them away from the pitcher, I could take full advantage of my power without affecting my swing, and so forth, and so forth.

I had heard it all before, but this time I listened. And, with Williams watching every move I made, I went down to Iron Mike for regular workouts, now learning not just to hit, but to hit home runs.

It paid off. You can't win baseball's triple crown without leading the league in home runs. In 1967 I led the league in batting at .326, in runs driven in with 121. And when I tied Harmon Killebrew of the Twins for the home-run leadership with 44, I had the triple crown.

I never would have won it without Williams.

CHAPTER 8

Going Nowhere

The Red Sox of 1961 and 1962 were a quiet club made up mostly of solid veterans who were in the business of playing ball. Win, lose, or draw, the locker room was like a morgue after every game. There was no exuberance, no cheering, no back-slapping when we won, no grumbling, no sulking, no anger when we lost. Schilling and I went for weeks at a time without talking to anyone except each other. We roomed together on the road, lockered side by side, warmed up together before ball games, sought each other out for meals and movies, and ignored everyone else. I didn't know the guy who lockered on the other side of me—I can't remember now who it was—and Schilling didn't know the guy on the other side of him. As far as we could tell, we were about the only ones who talked to each other. Sometimes, as we looked around the room, we marveled at the utter lack of communication among the other ballplayers. Some of them must have been friends, I suppose, but you'd never know it by their actions. They all seemed to be loners.

Not that they were bad guys, or unpleasant guys, or unfriendly guys. I never knew a warmer person than Frank Malzone, or a funnier one than Gene Conley, or a nicer one than Pete Runnels. But when they got into the Red Sox locker room they were like everyone else—not good, not bad. Just medium. Everyone was just medium, including Schilling and me. Heaven knows neither of us did anything to liven up the place. It was as if someone had hung huge SILENCE signs all over the walls. You walked in expecting to see a dead body on a slab, and you acted and talked as if it were right behind you. In two years I don't think I heard one solid, deep-throated yell. If I had, I'm sure I would have remembered it.

The first two months of the season were probably my worst in baseball. The big leagues frightened me, opposing pitchers handcuffed me, I was no ball of fire in the outfield, and the icy, indifferent atmosphere of the locker room robbed me of incentive. I wanted desperately to make the grade, but I also wanted to win, and we weren't winning. Manager Mike Higgins was nice to me, and I appreciated his confidence in me, but he was conservative and set in his ways. This would have been all right with a real good team or a consistently successful one, but we had too many problems.

The loss of Ted Williams meant tremendous loss of interest on the part of fans, for Williams was one of the greatest drawing cards in baseball history. Even with the team going nowhere, people came out to watch him. Now the team was still going nowhere, and there was no Williams. Attendance dropped, and empty seats in the stands were mute testimony to the growing indifference to the ball club.

Until Williams made his dramatic trip from Florida to help me, I was terribly discouraged. I picked up after he left, and finished pretty well, but I truly don't know how much I helped the ball club. We finished sixth in the first year of a ten-club American League, but two of the teams below us were expansion clubs, and a third was Kansas City, then hopelessly bad and destined to remain that way for several years.

The only comic relief was provided by Gene Conley, a 6-foot-8-inch pixie with a sly sense of humor, who was one of the world's few double-sport major-leaguers. In baseball's off-season he played basketball for the Boston Celtics. A wonderful guy with a friendly grin almost always decorating his face, he was the most popular man on the club.

He once showed up at the ball park after a two-day absence and said to Higgins, "Sorry, Mike, there was sickness in my family."

"That's too bad," said Higgins. "Who was sick?"

"Me," said Gene.

I probably was partly responsible for his most famous escapade. Gene was pitching a 4–4 ball game in New York when the Yankees got the bases loaded with two out. Somebody hit a high fly ball to left, I lost it in the sun, all three runs scored, and Gene, a great competitor despite his little foibles, blew up. When the next guy hit a homer, Higgins got him out of there.

Late in the afternoon the bus taking us to Newark Airport for the trip to Washington got snarled up in traffic. Gene got up and said, "Come on, Pumpsie, let's get out of here." He and Pumpsie Green, his pal, got off the bus, and we didn't see either of them for two days. When Pumpsie, who showed up first, arrived in Washington, he said, "Man, I've been living like a king. I had the biggest hotel suite in New York. I had the best wine, the best steaks. And Gene was going to take me to Israel."

"What were you going to Israel for?" somebody asked.

"You look at that big man," Pumpsie said, "and he says you're going to Israel, you're going to Israel. Besides, he was paying for everything."

Gene appeared the next day. He had bought a ticket to Israel but wasn't allowed on the plane because he had forgotten to get a passport.

My only souvenir from that 1961 season was a fear of flying I had never had before. Gary Geiger and Jackie Jensen were so terrified of air travel that it was the talk of the ball club. Whenever we stepped into a plane, the first thing we did was look around to see if they were aboard. They made the long trips, but went by train or drove whenever they could. After a while I began to wonder if maybe they had something, and pretty soon I was scared to death at the prospect of flying. It got so bad that one day at the Chicago airport I asked permission to rent a car and drive it to Boston. Higgins grabbed my arm, steered me aboard the plane, and said, "Sit down and relax. You're not driving anywhere." Jensen, who had already quit baseball once because of his fear of flying, finally had to quit permanently, but Geiger licked it. It took me a year to get over it, and even now I'm never quite comfortable in an airplane.

While the 1962 team was as indifferent as the 1961 club, there was one change for the worse, a sort of mass antagonism toward me. I first felt it in spring training, when other ballplayers started making remarks about my being the richest kid in town, and how I took the ball club for plenty, and all that sort of thing. Schilling and Fitzie kept telling me to ignore it, but it wasn't easy, especially when, after I got off to a good start, it was obvious that a lot of men on the bench were actually pulling against me.

One day Eddie Bressoud, who had come to us in a winter trade for Don Buddin, said, "Yaz, you're having a great year. You're a great young ballplayer and you'll be greater. Some of these chowderheads would like to see you collapse. Don't let them get you down. Just do your best and you'll be a big star long after they're forgotten."

Fitzie also encouraged me, especially in the late stages of the season, when it was obvious that the club would finish deep in the second division. By then there was so little interest on the part of the ballplayers that some didn't even look at the baseball standings when they read the sports pages.

"Don't worry about the others," Fitzie said. "Worry about yourself and your family. Hit for your wife and your kids. You don't have anything else to go for now. Guys like Malzone and Runnels and a few more are real pros. The better you do, the happier they are. Forget about the others. They're losers."

He looked hard at me, his Irish blue eyes bright as buttons. "And, Yaz, you're not a loser," he said. "Remember that. Because if you forget it you might let these guys pull you down to their level. You've got a big future. Don't give up because everyone else around here does."

By August I was going along nicely, batting around .300, hitting home runs at a rate that should give me 20 for the year, and working toward a total of 100 runs batted in. The last couple of months were usually my best, because I got stronger as the season progressed, but in mid-August I went into a slump and had trouble pulling out of it. Then I began feeling lousy physically. I played every day—didn't miss a game that whole 1962 season but things weren't right. My legs ached, I had back pains, and I felt so tired that all I wanted to do was sleep. The Red Sox sent me to Dr. Richard Wright, a specialist I had never met before, who today is one of my closest friends.

After giving me a routine physical examination, he said, "I think you're worrying too much about yourself. You've got all the ability in the world. Just go out and do the job."

"I don't understand why I'm so tired," I said. "Usually I feel great at this time of the year."

"If you don't feel any better soon, come back and see me again," he said. "But there doesn't seem to be anything seriously wrong."

I struggled through the rest of August, occasionally having a good day but going 1 for 4, 1 for 5 most of the time, batting in maybe half a dozen runs, not hitting a single homer, and feeling as weak as ever. I went back to Dr. Wright in the second week of September, and he began putting me through an intensive series of tests. I went to the hospital mornings and played ball afternoons or nights. About three days before the season ended he phoned to tell me I had jaundice.

"I still have a shot at a .300 batting average," I said. "Can I go for it or do you want me to quit?"

"You've gone this far," he said. "You might as well finish."

On the last day of the season I was batting .298, so if I got 3 for 3 against the Washington Senators I'd still get up to .300. I went into the game feeling terrible and came out feeling worse, because I couldn't hit the ball out of the infield against just average pitching. I ended up with a .296 average, 94 runs batted in, and 19 home runs, on a ball club that finished eighth. The only thing the Red Sox had to show for the season was Pete Runnels' second batting championship in three years.

Dr. Wright wouldn't let me go to school at all that year, and I never did return to Notre Dame. I went to Merrimack in subsequent years, but that winter I did nothing but eat, sleep, take pills, have periodic physical checkups, and loaf around the house. It took me until January to get rid of the last traces of yellow jaundice and start to put on some much-needed weight. I had finished the 1962 season at 160 pounds. The doctor wanted me to report for spring training at least 15 pounds heavier, which I did.

In the meantime the Red Sox made Mike Higgins general manager and named Johnny Pesky as the new bench manager. It was a tremendously popular move, for Pesky, a former Red Sox shortstop, had been living in the Boston suburb of Lynn for more than twenty years and had hundreds of personal friends all over New England.

I made a Red Sox promotional trip to Maine and New Hampshire with Pesky, whom I had never met before, and I was deeply impressed with him. He and I talked baseball constantly, about the team, what was wrong with it, what was needed to improve it, its future hopes and possibilities. Johnny, who had managed the top Red Sox farm club at Seattle the two previous years, knew more about those than I did. He had handled many of our younger players and felt he could light a fire under them to pull them out of the mass lethargy that seemed to have settled over the ball club. He infected me with his enthusiasm, and I went to Scottsdale for 1963 spring training happier than I had ever been about the prospects for the immediate future.

We had a new slugging first baseman in Dick Stuart, a promising pitching staff spearheaded by Bill Monbouquette, Dave Morehead, and Earl Wilson, a tremendous relief star in Dick Radatz, a coming young catcher in Bob Tillman, a young outfield, and what appeared to be a pretty good infield. Charlie Schilling was at second, Eddie Bressoud at short, Frank Malzone at third; I was in left, Gary Geiger and Roman Mejias were in center, and Lu Clinton was in right.

Pesky was running the show, and in early 1963 he really ran it. He had the whole team up when we arrived in Boston for the opening of the season. For the first time since I had been with the Red Sox, the boys were talking baseball, showing some life in the locker room, and acting like a single unit instead of a whole flock of small cliques with each group whispering in corners and looking suspiciously around at all the other cliques.

Soon after the season began, Fitzie came over to me and said, "Nobody's knocking you, Yaz. They all want you to have a good year because they know it will help them."

"That's good," I said. "I think we've got a chance to go places as long as we all pull together."

Schilling and I were still inseparable, but now we both paid more attention to the others in the clubhouse. Guys circulated, kidded each other, yelled back and forth across the locker room. When we won, you knew it—and you knew it when we lost, too. As the team moved, the hopelessness of the previous two years evaporated. The fans, smelling a big year, began coming out to the ball park in larger numbers, and by the end of May, Boston actually had a case of pennant fever.

Radatz was marvelous, the best relief pitcher in baseball. Almost every time he came into a ball game he blinded the opposition with fast balls, which he threw with no apparent effort, and he won or saved two games out of every three in which he appeared. Monbouquette, on his way to a 20-game season, did a great job. Tillman looked the part of the catcher the Red Sox had been trying to develop for years. Big Stu hit home runs like mad, and the rest of us all did our parts in the first two months of the season. By the end of June we were two games out of first place and talking pennant, while Johnny Pesky was the darling of his home-town fans.

What happened to us then is something I won't be able to explain to my dying day. We folded faster than I thought it possible for any team to fold. One week we were hot pennant contenders; the next we were out of it, dropping like a stone. We kept going down, down, down, with nobody on the ball club able to do anything to stop it. I sometimes wonder if anything could have been done, if we just weren't as good as we had looked. Yet I refuse to believe that. Granted, we were playing over our heads. Granted, we had the surprise element going for us. Granted, the other teams in the league got off to slower starts. But there must have been something somebody could have done to stop that terrible tailspin. This, I felt, was Pesky's job. He was the manager. He couldn't have won the pennant for us, but I thought he certainly could have prevented the collapse of morale that followed our nosedive to oblivion.

And the collapse of morale was total, with everyone bickering, criticizing, blaming others for his own shortcomings, falling back into those deadly cliques. Pesky, who had been the architect of our new-found spirit, practically lost control of the ball club.

A veteran utility man who had just joined the Red Sox was the best cardplayer I ever saw. One night he took a guy for several hundred dollars in a gin rummy game in the locker room. As he pocketed the money he said, "Nobody on a big-league ball club has a right to win or lose this much in a locker-room card game. If I were the manager, it would cost us each a thousand." He wasn't the manager, but he became the manager later, and one of his first moves was to ban high-stake card games. His name was Dick Williams.

As the team folded and the morale folded and the goodwill folded and the one-for-all-all-for-one spirit folded, smoldering dislikes rose to the surface and people started digging up buried hatchets. There were open arguments which sometimes stopped barely short of fist fights. There was bitterness that manifested itself in nasty cracks. When a guy did something wrong on the field, he heard about it in the worst possible way—by being laughed at. Everywhere you went in that locker room, you felt that someone had something to say about you that either had the whole clubhouse laughing or a few guys tittering. As it began happening to me, Schilling, Bressoud, and Fitzie worked on me to keep my own spirits up.

For I now had a shot at the American League batting title, and they didn't want me to blow it. Day after day Fitzie reminded me, "You're going to be the batting champion. Go out and get some hits. Don't think about anybody else. Think of yourself." Every so often Bressoud would say, "Yaz, go out and do it. Never mind the rest of us. We're dead. Save what you can for yourself." And Schilling told me over and over, "The hell with the others. They don't have anything at stake. You have. Get your hits and forget everyone else."

I did get my hits, but I made my share of mistakes. One night I blew a ball game by trying to throw directly home from deep left instead of throwing to the cutoff man. My throw was too high, it got by the catcher, and the winning run scored. When I went into the locker room somebody yelled, "Nice parachute throw, Yaz," and everybody laughed. I was wrong, of course. If I had let the cutoff man handle it, he might have caught the baserunner with a good relay, and maybe we could have saved the game. I never could laugh after a losing ball game, and I couldn't then. I clenched my fists and didn't calm down until Fitzie came over and murmured, "Cool it, Yaz."

Another time somebody called me a rally-killer because I was caught trying to stretch a double into a triple. I was wrong that time too. I should have settled for two bases, because I knew the outfielder had a good arm. I misjudged the play so badly he threw me out by ten feet. But I didn't like being called a rally-killer or having the whole locker room laugh at the way I ran bases.

When something like that happened I wished I could be like Dick Stuart, a happy-go-lucky guy, who didn't care what anyone said about him as long as he had his quota of home runs. He liked to talk about his power, the money he was making, his ability to hit any pitcher he faced, his home runs, his runs batted in, his fan popularity, but in such a way that nobody resented it. Big Stu was so good-natured that it was impossible to dislike him. And he didn't mind if you laughed at his fielding because he did himself. "I know I'm the world's worst fielder," he used to say, "but who gets paid for fielding? There isn't a great fielder in baseball getting the kind of dough I get for hitting."

He and Pesky got into ridiculous arguments, which sometimes drove the rest of us mad. They argued in buses, on airplanes, in locker rooms, in dugouts, bickering over whatever came into their heads. One night, after Big Stu belted one into the seats at Yankee Stadium, he yelled in the bus on the way to La Guardia, "How did you like that one, Pesky?"

"Anybody can hit home runs off these guys," Pesky said. "Back in my time we had pitchers like Newhouser and Feller and Trucks who could really throw hard. I'd like to see you hit one off them."

"You don't know anything about it," Stu said. "You couldn't hit anyhow."

"What do you mean I couldn't hit?" Pesky said. "I got two hundred hits in each of my first two years in the big leagues."

"Yah, what kind of hits?" Stu said. "Dunkers and bleeders and dribblers and Texas leaguers. You never hit five home runs in a season. I hit 'em forty at a time."

Most of the time Stu argued in good humor, but sometimes he really blew his stack, especially when Pesky benched him, which happened every so often. Stu, boiling after being benched in Chicago one time, waited until we got on the bus, then yelled, "What the hell right have you got to bench a $40,000 ballplayer?"

"I'm the manager, that's my right," Pesky yelled back.

"Whoever heard of a manager hitting the home runs I hit?" Stu said.

YAZ

"Your home runs don't mean a thing," Pesky said. "You lose more games than you win."

Stu changed the tone of his voice then as he said, "Say, John, I make $40,000. How much do you make, John—twenty? Maybe twenty-five? Is that what you make, John—twenty-five?"

And the argument degenerated into the same old pattern. I never could understand why Pesky took it. He was the manager, and for a while he had been a good one. I thought he could have shut Stuart up by taking away some of that $40,000 salary in fines. Then he would have regained the respect of us all and maybe salvaged something from the season's mess. In fairness to Pesky, I heard later that he actually did fine Stuart a few times, but the front office wouldn't back him up, which may or may not have been true. Whatever the story, it was a pretty sad situation.

The only thing that kept me going was the hope of winning the batting championship. With Fitzie giving me daily fight talks and Schilling reminding me that I had something to fight for even if nobody else did, I kept my average up in the .320s and .330s. In August my back began bothering me, and by the end of the month it hurt so much I couldn't bend down. Jack Fadden, the trainer, got me a big steel brace, which helped some, but I went through the last few weeks of the season on my nerve. My average slipped to .321, but nobody else did any better, and that saved me the batting crown.

But I got precious little satisfaction out of it, for the ball club finished seventh, and prospects for the immediate future weren't much better. On top of that, a series of unpleasant incidents temporarily embittered me toward everyone—the press, the fans, the ball club, the world, and Johnny Pesky, with whom it all started. Right after the season ended, Pesky admitted in a newspaper interview that as a rookie manager he had made a lot of mistakes, which he intended to correct in 1964. About a month later, in a banquet speech, I said, "We all made mistakes last year. I made mistakes, the ball club made mistakes, and"—remembering that Pesky had said this about himself—"the manager made mistakes."

· 128 ·

I'll admit it wasn't the most tactful thing to say, but I felt doubly justified in saying it, first because Pesky's mistakes were still fresh in my mind, and second because I was quoting him, rather than originating the remark myself. I certainly wouldn't have made it if he hadn't made it first. In any event, thanks largely to a Boston sports columnist who kept pointing up all of Pesky's virtues and my faults, a misunderstanding developed between Pesky and me. It wasn't straightened out as long as he continued to manage the ball club.

The repeated pounding from the Boston writer did not in itself sour me on the press, but I was upset over the failure of any of his colleagues to come to my defense. A typical example of how far afield this guy went in trying to make Pesky look good and me bad was his statement that, based on our records, Pesky was the better hitter. Perhaps he was right—Pesky's lifetime average of .307 is higher than mine today—but at that point it was unfair to me to base anything on our records, for Pesky's career was complete, and mine had hardly begun.

If anything like that came up now it wouldn't bother me. But in 1963 I was a sensitive twenty-four-year-old kid taking a bad beating from one newspaperman and not getting much help from the others. Instead of forgetting it, which I should have, I turned on a good part of the Boston press. I guess I was the toughest interview on the ball club for a couple of years, but I finally got over it.

The Pesky hassle and my disenchantment with the writers were only two of several factors that embittered me that year. My back didn't feel normal until December. I ate like a pig to put on weight and gained too much. And, although everyone thought I hadn't signed my 1964 contract because I was too busy with college classes, I actually was a holdout until the day spring training opened. I never admitted it because I didn't want to embarrass Tom Yawkey.

My 1963 salary had been $22,000, plus the last of five installments on my original bonus. Aside from wanting something to replace that bonus money, I felt my batting championship entitled me to a healthy raise, and I decided to ask for $35,000 for 1964. Up to then I had never had salary troubles, but up to then I had never dealt with Mike Higgins. Now, as general manager, he had the job of signing the ballplayers.

I didn't hear anything from the Red Sox until January, when Higgins, who lived in Dallas, came to Boston a couple of weeks in advance of the Boston Baseball Writers Dinner. One day a secretary called to tell me he wanted to see me, and we made an appointment. As we shook hands, Higgins said, "How are you, Yaz? How's the pheasant season?"

"Great," I said, not even aware that there was a pheasant season around Boston. "How was your winter in Texas?"

"Great," he said, lighting a cigarette. "I went fishing and did a little hunting."

He coughed, and he sat back in his chair, coughing and puffing, for about five minutes. He crushed out the butt and lit another, while I sat on my side of the desk waiting for him to make the first move. Finally he said, "Well, what do you think?"

"Well, Mike," I said, "I had a pretty good year. I won the batting title and I hit .321, and I think I'm worth $35,000 to the ball club next year."

He coughed and puffed and coughed and puffed for another five minutes, then said, "Yaz, did I tell you the time I hit .330 for Connie Mack? I hit 22 home runs and drove in 120 runs. I was making $4000 at the time, and when Connie offered me another thousand I grabbed it."

"What year was that, Mike?" I said.

"Oh, I dunno, nineteen thirty-four, thirty-five, something like that," he said.

"Well," I said, "this isn't nineteen thirty-four and you're not Connie Mack and I'm not you."

"We had a guy making around three thousand," Higgins said between coughs and puffs. "Wanted a raise so bad he held out right to spring training. He went up to the old man's nine-room suite overlooking the ocean and demanded another thousand. Connie says, 'The club ain't making any money, and I can't give out any raises.' The guy looks around the room at the nice furniture and out the window at the beautiful view of the ocean, puts his hand in his pocket, pulls out a fifty-cent piece, says, 'Mr. Mack, I feel sorry for you,' and he flips the fifty-cent piece at the old man." Higgins laughed until the tears came, took a puff, coughed, and said, "What do you think of that, Yaz? *He flipped a fifty-cent piece to the old man.*"

"I want $35,000, Mike," I said.

"Um," he said. He smoked and he coughed and he looked out the window, and after a while I got up.

"We didn't draw too well," Mike said. "Maybe if we draw better next year—"

"Thirty-five," I said. Then I walked out.

I went to Scottsdale without a contract and arrived on the day spring training began. Higgins called me right into his office and said, "Well, Yaz, what do you think?"

"I think I want $35,000," I said.

"I'll give you thirty," he said.

"Thirty-five," I said.

"Thirty-one."

"Thirty-five."

"Thirty-two."

"Thirty-five," I said.

"Thirty-three," Higgins said. "That's my limit."

He sat there puffing on his cigarette and coughing his deep cough, and I thought, *Oh, what the hell,* and settled for $33,000.

After that, everything went wrong. Pesky, with whom I was friendly during spring training, asked me to shift to center field. I knew my hitting would suffer, because it's much harder than left to play, but of course I agreed. I had a terrible weight problem, because I had eaten myself up to 195 pounds and couldn't shed the fat fast enough in the dry Arizona heat. I started the season 10 pounds overweight and didn't feel right for a month.

Charlie Schilling broke a bone in his hand, and when he got back Pesky kept him on the bench. When I realized Pesky wasn't going to let him try to win his second-base job back, I really got mad. By July I wasn't talking to Pesky, and soon he wouldn't talk to me because he said I didn't hustle for him. The fans started booing me every chance they got, until I finally said to Fitzie, "Now I see what happened to Ted Williams. The fans made life so miserable for him he turned against them. He wouldn't look at them or tip his cap. Now it's my turn."

"Don't talk like that, Yaz," Fitzie said. "Those fans are paying your salary."

"I don't have to tip my cap to them when they boo me," I said.

"Yes, you do," Fitzie said.

"Why?"

"Because Mr. Yawkey wants it that way."

I never again toyed with the idea of not tipping my cap to the fans.

One getaway night in Cleveland I had the flu and went out on the field with a temperature of 103 degrees. Since I wasn't speaking to Pesky, I told Coach Harry Malmberg, assuming he would pass the word along that I was too sick to play. Pesky started me, then kept me in while we were getting murdered by 8 or 9 to 1. Mad and miserable, I came to bat in the eighth inning with a man on first, hit a grounder to short, and was doubled up when, thinking two men were out instead of only one, I jogged to first base.

Back in Boston the next day, Pesky benched me. After sitting out three games I asked him why I wasn't playing.

"Because you dogged it in Cleveland," Pesky said. "You don't want to hustle, you don't have to play."

"I was sick," I said.

"Why didn't you tell somebody?" he said.

"I told Malmberg."

Pesky looked surprised and said, "He didn't tell me. I wouldn't have played you if I had known you were sick."

Realizing I should have told Pesky myself, I apologized, we shook hands, and that was that. A month later he was released, just before the season ended, and Billy Herman took his place. Pesky must have been happy to see the season end, but he wasn't any happier than I. Except for a fair .289 batting average, I found everything about the year horrible, including our eighth-place finish.

But the following January I had a speech all ready for Mike Higgins on why I should get a good raise: I was in the top ten among American League hitters, I had played center field all year, the cost of living had gone up 3.5 per cent, income taxes were getting higher, I had settled for less than I intended the year before, and so on.

Wait'll he says, "What do you think?" and sits back with his cough and his cigarette, I thought. *I'll tell him what I think.*

Except that he didn't say, "What do you think?" When I walked into his office, the first thing he said after shaking hands was, "Y'know, Yaz, after the year you had I could cut you."

I forgot about my speech and battled for what I already had and whatever little extra I could get. After a long, tough fight, I managed to talk Higgins into a $1000 raise, plus $4000 more if I had a good year. And I had to hold out again right up to the first day of spring training to get that.

CHAPTER 9

Who Wants
to Be Captain?

The ball players were happy about Herman's appointment because we were always happy when we got a new manager. This was a negative reaction, based on the theory that, since things couldn't be any worse, they'd have to get better. The two managers I had played for in Boston, Mike Higgins and Johnny Pesky, had failed for different reasons. Higgins was too conservative to experiment when things went wrong. Pesky had possibilities, but once he lost control of the ball club he could never get it back. He could still make somebody a good manager if he gets tough enough.

We knew Herman but didn't know what to expect of him. He was the only coach under Pesky who had also worked for Higgins. I had no personal feeling about him one way or the other. We had had a couple of run-ins over crossed signs when he was the third-base coach, but this happens every so often and I never considered it serious. All I cared about was whether or not he could lead us out of the wilderness we had been in ever since I joined the ball club.

I went in to see him the day he became the Red Sox manager and told him I'd do all I could to help.

"You've got to do more than you did this year," he said. "You've got to hustle and break your neck, which you know you didn't."

"I know I didn't get the most out of myself," I said. "I reported in lousy condition and that's why I had a lousy season. Next year I'll know better. I'll report at 185 instead of 195, and I'll come to play ball."

"I know you're a great ballplayer," Herman said. "You've had an off year, but now that's all over. If we all pull together we can make it big."

Wonderful! Great! Lovely! The ball club is great, the manager is great, the front office is great, I'm great, we're all great. The new leaf is turned over, and now we're ready for action.

Herman's first move was to get rid of Dick Stuart. The Red Sox traded him to the Phillies for Dennis Bennett, which brought some of the press down on our necks, for Bennett had a sore arm and Stuart represented about thirty-five homers and a hundred runs batted in every year. The ballplayers greeted the deal with mixed emotions. We all got a kick out of Stu, yet we knew he could be a demoralizing influence.

Our 1965 prospects actually weren't bad. We had two great rookies in Rico Petrocelli and Jim Lonborg. We had the best young right-handed power hitter in baseball in Tony Conigliaro, a rookie the year before. In Dalton Jones we had another second-year man who could hit and who could play anywhere in the infield. Lonborg, Monbouquette, Radatz, Morehead, and Earl Wilson gave us the backbone of a pretty good pitching staff.

Our catching was only fair, and we were far from set in the infield. Lee Thomas, the first baseman, was really an outfielder. I thought Charlie Schilling would have fitted right back in at second base, but maybe I was prejudiced because we were so close. In any event, Herman gave him no more chance to get back than Pesky had. Felix Mantilla, a right-handed power hitter but not much of a fielder, played second base most of the season. We also needed help in center field.

We weren't going to win a pennant with this club, but we didn't figure to end up anywhere near the cellar either. I thought it was the best team since I had been with the Red Sox, at least as good as the 1963 club, which Pesky had going like mad for a while. It was a younger team than Pesky's, and a more promising one. With a few breaks and good leadership, we could finish in the first division.

Although I had no beef with Herman in 1965, there was one thing that bothered me about him when we first reported for spring training. This man was a golf nut. He never went anywhere without his clubs, which were always in sight in his office. He ran easy training sessions, finished them early, had short post-workout press conferences, then went off to the nearest course. He talked golf morning, noon, and night, which was great if you liked golf. I didn't at the time, although I do now.

I got off to a great start, but the ball club didn't. Six weeks after the season began, I was hitting around .350 and having visions of another batting title, but the team was down around eighth place. I hit for the cycle against the Tigers in Boston one night in May, with two homers, a single, a double, and a triple, for 14 total bases.

The next night I was going in to second base when my spikes caught and I got pretty badly hurt crashing into Jake Wood, the Tiger second baseman. His knee went hard into my ribs, and I was in so much pain I had to get out of there. But when nothing showed in a locker-room examination I was told to go home, take it easy, and call in if the pain got any worse.

The next night I felt well enough to suggest to Carol that we go out for dinner, but just before we were supposed to leave I passed blood. Scared to death, I phoned Dr. Wright, who told me he'd meet me at the hospital in half an hour, and to be sure that Carol did the driving. I had two broken ribs and a crushed kidney that bled so steadily Dr. Wright said I'd have to lie immobile for four days. "If it doesn't stop then," he said, "we'll operate."

It didn't stop until the end of the fourth day, and I still couldn't move for three days more. Altogether, I spent nine days in the hospital, nine days during which I would have gone nuts if it hadn't been for Tom Yawkey. He came to see me every day, spending hours with me, talking about everything under the sun —baseball, fishing, hunting, people we knew, my family, potato farming, the future. Dreadful as those nine days were, I look back on them now with a touch of longing, for they gave me the only chance I ever had to get to know the man who had already paid me about a quarter of a million dollars in salaries and bonuses.

We talked mostly about me, because he kept drawing me out, but sometimes we talked about him too. One day he said, "Yaz, you have no idea what it would mean to me to win a pennant— just one pennant. We won in 1946 and came close in 1948 and 1949, but we haven't been anywhere near since."

"Mr. Yawkey," I said, "I like to win too. I know one guy can't win a pennant, but we have good kids coming up and more developing in the farm system. One of these days the whole ball club will jell. And I want to be a part of it."

"I'm sure you will be, Yaz," he said. "You're our key man. But you're right. One man can't do it. It must be a team effort."

After he left I used to lie still in that hospital bed and think, *What a thrill it would be to give that man the pennant that means so much to him. I wish I could help give him a whole flock of pennants. I wish . . .*

And sometimes I realized you can't wish yourself to a pennant. Pennants are won on the ball field, not in people's minds or on hospital beds. Everyone who knew Yawkey, and thousands who didn't, wanted to see his Red Sox win a pennant, but there had never been the right combination—the right ballplayers, the right manager, the right attitude, the right desire. They all had to be there at once. They hadn't been in my time, and they certainly weren't now.

Carol and my dad picked me up at the hospital and drove me home on a Sunday. I spent the day walking to try to get some strength back into my legs. I walked some more Monday morning, and Monday afternoon was at the ball park taking batting practice. The doctor told me to take it easy, but I had taken it easy long enough and now I insisted on playing. Jack Fadden, the trainer, said I was crazy, but he finally taped up my ribs, and I was in Tuesday's ball game. I played all week but didn't feel right; then on Saturday I started bleeding internally again. When the ball club left on a road trip after Sunday's game, I was home in bed, this time with strict orders to do nothing without the doctor's permission.

It was another week before I could play. I started as if I had never been out, and my batting average stayed up in the .340s. I was leading the league and looking forward to the All-Star Game when I tore a leg muscle running out a pop fly. I hit it off Sonny Siebert of the Cleveland Indians, ran hard down the line, rounded first, streaked for second, and suddenly pulled up short with a stabbing pain that felt as if my left leg was dropping off. Down I went, and they had to carry me off in a stretcher. Instead of playing in the All-Star Game, I spent the next week and a half with Carol and the kids at Bridgehampton, where I could soak up sun on the beach. My injuries caused me to miss 27 of our first 81 games.

In the meantime, all sorts of things were happening to the ball club. We ended the week before the All-Star break with a 6-game losing streak, giving us 30 defeats in the 40 games we had played since Memorial Day. Billy Herman finally pulled a surprise bed check in Baltimore. He fined everyone he caught and announced there would be more bed checks before the season ended. It was a classic case of locking the barn door after the horse was stolen. It was too late. Instead of fighting for the first division, we were battling to stay out of the cellar.

As the team continued to lose, the Boston newspapers sniped at everyone from Yawkey down. Somebody started a rumor that he wanted to sell the ball club, a story I found completely mystifying in view of what I knew of the man. He never had either the desire or the intention of selling, for baseball was his greatest pleasure, and he still clung to the hope that some day the Red Sox would deliver the pennant he wanted so badly. I don't know where the rumor began or why it spread, but it went out on the wire services, because I first read about it in the New York papers. It didn't die down until Yawkey categorically announced there was nothing to it.

Things were going so badly it was obvious we needed a major change. It came in September, when Yawkey let Mike Higgins go and installed Dick O'Connell as the general manager. From that moment on, I knew that sooner or later we would be all right. O'Connell, the Red Sox business manager for years, was a sound executive who knew exactly where he was going and how to get there. It was he who started the chain of events that led to our astounding success in 1967. He brought in Haywood Sullivan as director of player personnel, made or approved a dozen deals that helped us, and finally appointed Dick Williams manager.

But first he gave Billy Herman a chance to do what he could with the ball club. Herman had a two-year contract, carrying through the 1966 season, a circumstance which might have made Billy a little careless about the way he talked. Remember, he was a Higgins man—he had coached under Higgins as manager and he had managed under Higgins as general manager. A few days after O'Connell moved up, I was playing pinochle in an airplane with Herman, Billy Gardner, and Pete Runnels, when Herman began to knock O'Connell. He kept it up, while I didn't say a word. But Herman must have known I resented it, because he never again did it in my presence.

We lost a hundred games and finished ninth, forty games behind the pennant-winning Twins and only three in front of last-place Kansas City. My own hopes for salvaging anything from the season went out the window with that muscle pull I suffered against Cleveland. My left leg is the one I push off when I hit, and it wasn't completely healed until after Labor Day. My average dipped and I finished at .312, second behind Tony Oliva of the Twins, who won the batting title at .321.

The Red Sox shifted from Scottsdale to Winter Haven, Florida, for spring training in 1966, a season that began on a bizarre note and ended on a hopeful one. The bizarre note was provided by the ballplayers, who got permission from Herman to have a meeting without him or the coaches. The idea was conceived by Dick Radatz during a barbecue welcoming the ball club to Winter Haven. Some people thought I had something to do with it, but, since I didn't even go to the barbecue, I was probably the last to find out. Charlie Schilling told me on the way to the ball park the next morning.

"How can we have a meeting without the manager?" I said.

"Don't ask me," Schilling said. "Nobody else did, and I'm the player representative."

Radatz ran the meeting, which was held instead of practice that morning. Everybody on the squad was there, including maybe forty rookies who, not having been with the team in 1965, didn't know what had gone on then and had no idea of what everyone else was talking about. When he started the meeting, Radatz said something like, "We can say what we like, and everyone will have a chance to speak. Now here's Billy."

Everyone clapped and cheered when Herman walked in. As he bowed, two golf balls dropped out of his pocket and bounced around the floor. After picking them up he said, "I'm happy you fellows are having this meeting. I'm sure it will clear the air and we'll do a real good job this year." He talked a few more minutes, then left us to ourselves.

One by one, guys stood up and talked about working hard and obeying the rules and all that sort of thing. A few let their hair down, admitting past transgressions and promising not to repeat them. There was a lot of talk about rules—in fact, a whole code of rules was drawn up, and everyone was asked to live up to them and to make sure everyone else lived up to them. It was also agreed we should have a captain. Schilling and I sat and listened to all this, wondering where it would end—or, for that matter, if it would ever begin. Finally Radatz asked me to speak.

"Well," I said, "I suppose it's all right for everybody to get religion and clear the air and promise to turn over a new leaf, but I don't think this is the way to do it. It isn't up to us to set the rules. That's the manager's job. And it's not up to us to enforce them. That's both the manager's and the coaches' job. We can't police each other or spy on each other or turn each other in.

"We have one job," I went on, "and this is to work like hell down here, get ourselves into the best possible shape, keep ourselves that way during the season, and hustle every minute of every ball game. But we can't run the ball club. And we shouldn't even be meeting like this without the manager or the coaches."

I talked a little about the rules they had set up, told the guys the only rules I'd obey were those set by the manager, and then I sat down. There was a lot more discussion, which didn't make much sense to me, and after an hour and a half Herman and the coaches returned and we all went out on the field for a workout.

If the meeting accomplished anything, it started everyone working overtime for about a week. I think Radatz and the others really hoped to change the team's defeatist attitude, and I was glad to cooperate, but I still felt this was Herman's job, not ours. I wasn't surprised that all those good resolutions were kept for only a week. Once their first impact had worn off, everyone went back to his old habits. It isn't easy to work hard in spring training. The only guys who did were the rookies and those veterans who always had anyhow. So by the time we broke camp at Winter Haven, all the promises made at our managerless, coachless revival meeting had been broken, and nothing whatever had been gained.

Charlie Schilling was traded to the Twins while we were on our way north, and that really soured me on Herman. He had never liked Schilling as a ballplayer, even though Charlie had been a good second baseman who could hit big-league pitching, before he hurt his hand. Whether or not that permanently impaired his efficiency I don't know, but I do know that my resentment against Herman was deeper than my feeling against Pesky. Pesky hadn't given Schilling much of a chance either, but at least he had kept the guy. The whole Schilling situation was a very personal thing to me.

I was still upset about Charlie's departure when the team met in Boston on the day before the 1966 season began, this time to elect a captain. I didn't think much of the idea, because I felt the captain, if any, should be chosen by the manager. Since only two guys agreed with me, I was heavily outvoted. To make matters worse, I was the guy elected—in a secret ballot, with neither the manager nor the coaches present. I didn't want the job but couldn't very well refuse it without causing trouble. I took it for the sake of harmony, and to this day I wish I hadn't.

For now I found myself in the middle of every hassle, every disagreement, every beef and gripe and complaint on a ball club which had specialized in hassles, disagreements, beefs, gripes, and complaints for years. If a guy needed money, he came to me. If a guy thought he was unfairly fined, he came to me. If a guy wasn't playing and thought he ought to be, he came to me. If a guy was worried about being traded, he came to me. If a guy got out of bed on the wrong side in the morning, he came to me.

Yet nobody really trusted me. Because I was supposed to be the go-between between the ballplayers and the manager, everybody thought I had a special "in" with Herman and the front office. Right after I was elected somebody had the idea of my consulting Herman every day to see if there was anything he wanted me to relay to the players. This was exactly the sort of thing I had objected to in the first place, for it widened the gap between manager and players. Herman had never communicated much with the players anyhow. Now he practically stopped altogether. If he had anything to tell them, he did it through me.

But not for long. After about a week I stopped seeing him every day because I thought the whole idea was silly. The last thing I wanted was to get mixed up in clubhouse politics. We had a manager who was supposed to be in charge. We had coaches who were supposed to carry out the manager's orders. We had a player representative who was supposed to protect the players' interests. What did we need a captain for, and why should it be me?

Two weeks after the season began, Herman did an astounding thing. When we arrived in Anaheim after losing two games in a row in Kansas City, he called a meeting in the locker room, stood up in front of us all, and said—and I can't print his exact words —"I don't care about any one of you guys. The only person I care about is Billy Herman. Nobody around here is going to do anything to jeopardize my job, and don't you forget it." Then he turned around and walked into his office.

I don't know why he was so bitter. Maybe he thought he could fire us up this way. The club was going badly and he undoubtedly was upset. I could see a manager getting mad, bawling everybody out, pointing out mistakes and demanding they be corrected. I could see a manager blowing his stack because the team was losing. But it didn't seem right for a manager to tell a group of ballplayers, several of them rookies, that he didn't care about any of them and that nobody was going to jeopardize his job. Everyone was so sore and resentful that I went in to see Herman the next day and said, "Billy, you couldn't have meant what you said yesterday. You must be sorry. Do you want me to apologize for you to the ball club?"

He agreed, so I called a meeting and told everyone that Herman was sorry for what he had said, that the only reason he said it was that we were losing and he wanted to get us mad enough to win. I don't think the apology did much good because the wrong guy made it, but even if Herman had made it himself, it was too late to help much.

Of all the Red Sox ballplayers, the one Herman disliked most was Rico Petrocelli, a fine young shortstop so sensitive that he needed continual assurance of his great ability. Petrocelli, who really didn't know his own strength, had to be handled with kid gloves, for one bad day would get him down for a week. Herman was tough with him, treating him with icy scorn, especially when Petrocelli, who suffered a variety of minor but nagging ailments that year, was unable to play at 100-per-cent efficiency. Herman thought he was loafing and openly told newspapermen he had a shortstop who didn't want to play ball.

Petrocelli's locker was right near mine. I tried to help him because he obviously needed understanding badly and wasn't getting any from Herman. One day, after Herman had let him stew on the bench for a while, Petrocelli came over to me and said, "Yaz, I can't make it. I'm going to quit."

"Don't be ridiculous," I said. "You'll be the best shortstop in the business in a couple of years."

"Herman doesn't think so," he said.

"I don't care what Herman thinks," I said. "You've got it and you're going to make it big."

After that Rico often threatened to quit, not because he intended to but because he needed somebody to tell him not to. He was a born worrier, and for a time he really had something to worry about. His wife was sick, and when he came to the ball park he imagined all sorts of terrible things happening to her. One day, soon after the 1966 season opened, he disappeared right in the middle of a ball game and went home because he was sure she needed him. After the game Petrocelli's walkout was the talk of the locker room. Leaving a game without permission is the most unforgivable of all baseball offenses, and few ballplayers have ever done it.

I was about to go home after the game when I got word that Mr. Yawkey wanted to see me. When I arrived at his office things were pretty hectic. Herman was demanding that Petrocelli be traded on the spot. O'Connell was sitting at a desk, calling one hospital after another, trying to locate Rico and his wife. Mr. and Mrs. Yawkey were both there, talking quietly about what had happened.

"You know this boy, Yaz," Yawkey said. "Why would he do something like this?"

"Something has to be bothering him," I said. "The kid's scared —scared he won't make the ball club, scared he's not doing the job, scared for his wife. She's been sick, you know."

"I know," Yawkey said. "But to walk out during a game—" He shook his head.

"Well, Mr. Yawkey," I said, "if he had any idea how serious it was, he'd never have done it. But Rico is that way. He gets one thing on his mind and forgets everything else. He was worried about his wife, and nothing else counted."

"Trade him," Herman said. "Get rid of him. He doesn't want to play ball."

Right about then O'Connell located the Petrocellis at the Union Hospital in Peabody. It turned out that Rico had found his wife writhing in pain on the kitchen floor and rushed her to the hospital. She had some sort of stomach ailment and, although not in danger, would have had to endure the pain for several more hours if Rico hadn't got there. The Yawkeys thanked me for coming, and I went home. A day or two later Herman told the writers he had fined Rico $1000, which was just about one-ninth of Rico's salary. I thought that was pretty stiff, but of course it was Herman's right to set any punishment he thought fitted the crime.

My own relations with Herman deteriorated as the season progressed. One night in New York I went out for a hamburger around the corner from the hotel and ran into a couple of Boston baseball writers who were very close to Herman.

"Yaz," one of them said, "you might as well know that Herman wants to trade you."

"Why would Herman want to trade me?" I asked.

"Maybe because he doesn't like you," was the reply.

I didn't really pay much attention, but a month later I was sitting with the same guys in the Chicago airport waiting for a plane to Minneapolis when one of them said, "Herman's still trying to get rid of you." Then it began to bother me. I loved Boston, the Red Sox, and Tom Yawkey; Carol and I had many friends in and around town; we had just bought a new home in Lynnfield; and the last thing we wanted was to go anywhere else. If Herman really intended to trade me, I had to find out why. But before I could say anything to him, he came to me one day in Washington.

"Yaz," he said, "you're not putting out at all, and I know it."

"Well," I said, "I know I'm putting out, but if you feel that way, I can't stop you."

"One of us isn't going to be here next year," he said. "I think I'm going to be here and you're not."

"I know all about that," I said. "Some of the writers told me. I started my big-league career here, and I've always wanted to end it here, but if you're here next year I don't want to be."

When I got home from that trip, I told Carol, "We've got to be ready. There's a good chance I'll be traded."

"What are we going to do?" she said. "We don't even know where we're going."

We didn't know, but other people seemed to. Almost every day some writer was sending me somewhere—to California, to Detroit, to Houston, to New York, to Chicago—and every time I read a rumor about being traded I squirmed. Yet the more I thought about it, the less reason I could find for the Red Sox to keep me. They weren't going anywhere, and neither was I. While the team floundered around near the cellar I was having my worst season since 1961, my rookie year. I was collecting the highest salary on the club and batting under .280. And I obviously wasn't getting along with the manager.

There really was no reason for the club to do so poorly. Once again we had two great young rookies, George Scott at first base and Joe Foy at third. All Petrocelli needed to be a star was confidence, for he was an outstanding fielder with a great arm and could hit with power. Tony Conigliaro, the 1965 home-run king, was on his way toward becoming a superstar, and our pitching was getting better all the time. We were weak at second base and in center field, and we needed help behind the plate, but we were a far better ball club than the standings showed. We shouldn't have been anywhere near the cellar, for we had a young team with a lot of potential. Some of it showed during the second half of the season, when we won more games than we lost.

But we still weren't going anywhere. When we landed in the cellar shortly after Labor Day, the Red Sox suddenly fired Billy Herman, replacing him with Pete Runnels as interim manager until the end of the season. From then on, all we thought about was the new manager, and the players speculated as much as everyone else. Even though we finished ninth again, only half a game out of the cellar, we knew the right man could take us a long way.

On the day after the season ended, Dick O'Connell and Haywood Sullivan presented the new manager to the Boston press. He was Dick Williams, a teammate of mine for two years under Johnny Pesky, a bright, tough needler who lived, breathed, ate, talked, thought, and slept baseball, and who had won two International League playoffs in a row as manager of the Red Sox farm club in Toronto. He knew our kids and had managed most of them. He knew our ball club because he had played on it only two years before. He knew our weaknesses because he had seen them himself and often talked about them. He knew what we had and what we lacked and what had to be done to make up for that lack. Although young (he was only ten years older than I) and inexperienced (he had never managed before going to Toronto), he looked, to those of us who knew him, a fine choice, maybe the perfect choice for our ball club.

CHAPTER 10

Trade Rumors

After Herman left I thought all the trade rumors about me would stop, but they seemed to increase. Almost every day somebody had a story about where I might be going, when, and for whom. No one really knew anything, but many close Red Sox observers apparently took it as a matter of course that I wouldn't be around very long. I couldn't understand why. With Herman gone, there was no reason to believe I'd be traded, because I didn't know of anyone else in the organization who wanted to get rid of me, but you can't read and hear so much about yourself without feeling that where there's that much smoke there must be some fire.

All my worries should have ended on the last day of the 1966 season, when Mr. Yawkey sent for me and said, "Yaz, don't worry about being traded. I'm not going to trade you unless some fantastic deal comes along."

"Like what?" I said.

"Oh, the kind that couldn't happen," he said. "A superstar offer like Juan Marichal or Bob Clemente. But ball clubs don't trade players like that, and we're not going to trade you. Just have a good winter and don't believe what you read or hear, because you'll be with us next year and, I hope, for a lot of years after that."

The very next day the rumors began all over again after Dick Williams' first press conference. Somebody asked him whether or not he would have a captain.

"Definitely not," he said. "We have a manager and four coaches. That's all the chiefs we need. Everyone else will be Indians."

People took this as a slap at me. The new manager starts right off by putting Yaz in his place, they said. Maybe the new manager doesn't like Yaz. Maybe the new manager wants to trade Yaz. Yaz has been on the block all summer and he'll still be on the block.

What people didn't know was that Dick O'Connell and I had had a talk about the captaincy immediately after Herman left.

"If you want it, you can keep it," he had told me.

"I don't want it," I said. "I'll be glad to get rid of it."

So even before Williams became the manager it had been decided by mutual consent that I would no longer be the captain. But since this was known only to O'Connell and me (I'm not sure even Williams knew), everybody made a big thing of Williams' announcement. And, partly on the basis of it, everybody continued to trade me—everybody but the Red Sox, that is.

There are people who believe everything they see in print, and if it's repeated often enough in print even those who should know better begin to believe it. That was what happened to me during the fall of 1966. Interleague trading was on, and every club in the two big leagues was looking for deals that might help. O'Connell and Sullivan practically lived on the telephone, either dreaming up possible deals or discussing somebody else's dreams on the subject.

They're all after Yaz, the papers proclaimed. *We're on the verge of something big. Yaz is going. The Red Sox definitely have him on the market*. And so forth.

This went on day after day, while Carol and I went nuts in

our new house in Lynnfield. Although I knew somebody would phone to tell me if I really had been traded, the first thing we did every morning was study the newspapers. One of us always caught the sports broadcasts from the major radio and TV stations all day, and we couldn't wait for the evening papers. It got to be an obsession. Either she or I kept bringing the subject up, and neither of us could talk about much of anything else.

"What are we going to do if we're traded?" she said one night.

"I don't know," I said. "I just don't know."

"Didn't Mr. Yawkey say you wouldn't be?"

"Not unless a very good deal came along," I said. "And he didn't expect one. He practically promised I'd stay, but—well—I hear all these rumors and I don't know what to think."

"Carl," she said, "I don't want to leave here."

"Neither do I," I said. "But if we have to go anywhere, I hope it's LA. There's a lot doing on the West Coast. The change might be good for me. Or New York. That would be my second choice—the Yankees maybe. If I have a good year with them, I can make a lot of money."

"What if we have to go somewhere else?"

"We won't go anywhere else," I said.

"How do you know?"

"I'll just refuse to go," I said. "If they trade me anywhere else but Los Angeles or New York, I'll quit."

"How can you quit?" she said.

"I just will, that's all," I said.

The discussion was ridiculous, but when you get desperate you say ridiculous things. I was scared, upset, apprehensive. I needed a good shot of confidence from somebody like Yawkey or O'Connell. Those newspaper stories were getting me down—farther and farther down as the autumn progressed. It got so bad I lay awake nights wondering what would happen, where we were going, whether we should sell the house or keep it, whether we would move permanently or stay around the Boston area, where the children would go to school, where I could find a decent job if I was traded to the wrong team and quit, where else in the world we would be nearly as happy as we were in Boston.

While I was worrying myself to a frazzle, I realized I'd have to do something to keep in shape. I worked in the off-season in the Boston office of the Portland Printing Corporation, but my hours were flexible and I could make any arrangements I wanted to. I decided to take light workouts in the late afternoon, increasing them as spring training approached, so I'd be ready when it was time to go south—if that was where I was going.

One day while sitting around the Colonial Inn in Lynnfield with George Page, the owner, and Mel Massucco, who worked with him, I mentioned something about keeping in shape.

"Work out here," Page said. "Gene Berde, who runs our health club, used to coach the Hungarian Olympic boxing team. He'll get you into shape faster than anyone you ever saw. Come on and meet him."

The next thing I knew, I was shaking hands with a gnome of a man, short and slight, with bright blue eyes and a constant smile playing about his lips. After Page introduced us Berde said, "So you're the great baseball star Carl Yastrzemski." He reached out and prodded me in the stomach. "You think you're in shape?" he said.

"Well," I said, "I'm not in bad shape."

"Huh," he said, "you the big baseball player. You the big champion. You the best one on the team. You can't even run a hundred yards. You no athlete. In my country you are nothing, because in this shape you are not even a third-class athlete. All right. You do what I say. I put you in shape."

I got into a pair of shorts, and he stood in front of me and said, "Take a deep breath." I took a breath and he said, "Ha, you can't even breathe right. You breathe with your mouth. You should breathe with your lungs."

He began putting me through calisthenics, stopping me for deep breathing after each exercise. In ten minutes I was dead, but Berde, who did everything with me, was fresh and sharp.

"You're soft," he said. "You have a good body, but you're flabby. You have no resistance. You are not athlete in my country in this shape. I am surprised in United States you are one of the biggest athletes, your picture in the paper every day almost. The children look at you like you were a god."

Between puffs I said, "How old are you?"

"Sixty-one," he said.

"How much do you weigh?"

"Hundred fifty."

"How tall?"

"Five six."

"I'm twenty-seven, six feet, and a hundred and eighty-five pounds," I said. "How come ten minutes of this knocks me out and doesn't bother you at all?"

"Your condition," he said. "It's bad. Look. Jump rope."

He handed me a rope and I started jumping like a boxer. Thirty seconds later I collapsed.

"Half a minute," he said, "and look at you. You the great athlete. You should be ashamed. Look."

He jumped rope for three minutes without even working up a sweat, while I sat on a chair, gasping and marveling. Then he dropped the rope and pointed to a treadmill device. I dragged myself over to it, tried to run, and quit after twenty seconds.

"I can't do any more, Gene," I said. "I'll be back tomorrow."

"Okay," he said. "I am here."

He told me later he didn't think I'd ever be back, but I made it the next day and the day after that and almost all the other days for the rest of the winter. One day he said, "Carl, how much your salary now? Fifty thousand? Sixty thousand? Next year you get double."

"You're crazy," I said.

"Not crazy," he said. "You watch. You get it. You do what I tell you, you be strong and you get it."

I did what he told me. In six weeks it took more time to tire me out, and I felt better mentally as well as physically. As the winter days went by without any trade news, I breathed a little easier. I stopped reaching for the papers, catching all the sports broadcasts, talking about where we would go and what we'd do if it wasn't to the right city. The interleague trading deadline came and went without my going over to the National League. If the Red Sox were going to trade me, it would have to be to an American League team.

In January I had a call from Dick O'Connell, who wanted to see me about my 1967 contract. When I went up there we didn't even talk about money at first.

"Yaz," he said, "you have all the ability in the world. Why can't we get it out of you?"

"Maybe you will this year," I said. "I've been taking these exercises." I told him about Gene Berde, then said, "I feel great mentally and physically."

"That's fine," O'Connell said. "But you have to quit worrying about everything that's going on. You worry about the other ballplayers, you worry about the manager and the decisions he makes, you worry about the front office, you worry about the ball club. Forget it. Your main thing is to go out and play left field. That's it—all of it. Give a hundred per cent on the ball field, take your shower, get dressed, and go home and forget about the game. Even if we lose, even if we finish in the cellar, don't worry. You give your hundred per cent, and that's all we ask of you. Somebody makes an error and blows a ball game, let him worry about it. Don't you. A pitcher hits a batter with the bases loaded and we lose the game, that's his worry. Not yours. All right?"

"All right," I said.

"What do you think would be a fair contract for you?" he said.

I told him. I didn't go in for a big long discussion of what I did right and how much more I deserved and why. I just named a figure, and he said okay. Then he said, "Yaz, there's a lot of rumors about you in the papers and on the air. I suppose you've been worrying about that too."

"A little," I said. It was the understatement of the year.

"Well," O'Connell said, "I can tell you that at no time did we offer you for trade."

"Really?"

"Really," he said. "Clubs have asked about you. During inter-league trading the Phillies kept calling us with offers. The White Sox and the Angels still call us almost every day. We talk and talk and somebody mentions you and I say, 'Forget it. We're not trading him.' Do you understand that?"

"I do now," I said. "I just didn't know what to think during the winter."

"Mr. Yawkey told you he wouldn't trade you," O'Connell said.

"Well," I said, "he said if some big superstar deal was offered—"

"But he didn't expect one. Nobody does. Remember, Yaz, *we're not trading you.* Read all you want, listen all you want, but don't worry. All right?"

"All right," I said.

I walked out on air, for O'Connell had given me just the lift I needed. All the worrying and sleepless nights and mental threats about what I'd do if I were traded somewhere I didn't want to go had been unnecessary. The Red Sox wouldn't trade me, never intended to trade me, weren't interested in talking about trading me, and O'Connell's assurance was just what I needed. Back home, I told Carol, "I'll break my back for those guys. I'll have the greatest year of my life. You watch."

By late February, when it was time to go south, I was in marvelous condition. After three months with Gene Berde, I could do everything he could: working with wall pulleys, stretching on a Swedish wall ladder, running the treadmill, riding the bicycle, jumping rope—I could do it for five minutes—doing high kicks and knee bends and pushups and arm stretching, tossing a medicine ball, doing forward and backward somersaults, topping everything with twenty 60-yard sprints. Toward the end I was swinging a heavy bat, getting used to the feel of it.

Often my partner in these workouts was Governor John A. Volpe of Massachusetts. He was fifty-eight then, but looked fifteen years younger, for he had been working out with Gene Berde since 1962. I imagine he's in the best physical shape of any American governor, regardless of age. He and I still work out together, and, although I'm thirty years younger, there's nothing in Berde's routine I can do that he can't do as well or for as long.

The routine was a terrible grind but worth every minute, for it gave me mental confidence, rigid control of my body, quickness, coordination, and endurance. I couldn't wait to get to Winter Haven, couldn't wait to start spring training, couldn't wait to play ball. In other years I had always worried that I wouldn't get into shape in time for the opening of the season, but not this time. When I went to Florida, I was really ready.

I drove down with Frank Malzone, now a special scout for the Red Sox. On the way we decided to get an apartment, and Frank would move out when Carol came down the following week to spend two weeks with me. I paid rent for the entire period of spring training.

Everybody was waiting for my first meeting with the new manager, Dick Williams, figuring there'd be a blowup over my lost captaincy and maybe over a few other things. Williams had a rule that single ballplayers and married ones without their wives were to stay in the club's headquarters hotel. He had enforced it with everyone else, and the question in the minds of observers was whether or not he would enforce it with me.

He called me into his office my first day at the ball park and said, "Yaz, is Carol coming down?"

"In about a week," I said.

"Okay," he said. "That's all I want to know."

"Dick," I said, "there's a couple of other things I'd like to talk about."

"Go ahead," he said.

"We've had a lot of new deals since I've been with the club," I said. "None of them worked, for one reason or another. Just because we never won anything doesn't mean I'm used to losing or like it. I'll do anything you say. If you want me to bunt I'll bunt. If you want me to hit and run I'll hit and run. If you want me to steal I'll steal. I think we've got pretty good talent here. I want to play baseball and I want to win. You give the orders and I'll obey them."

"That's fine," he said. "I know you and I respect you for what you are. People blamed you for some of the things that went wrong around here, and I know none of it was your fault. You're a winner, you're my kind of ballplayer."

"I started my career in Boston," I said. "It's the only choice I ever had, and once I chose it I was never sorry. My home, my friends, my children's roots are there. My wife and I have always loved it. We don't ever want to leave."

"I know you," Williams said again. "And you know me. You give me your best and we'll get along fine."

"Okay," I said, and after a little more talk I left. It had been a rather long huddle, and I knew people wondered just what happened. Our discussion had been strictly about baseball, friendly if not warm, without the slightest misunderstanding. When I walked out of Dick's office that day I knew just what he wanted of me and he knew just what to expect. He would be tough, but nobody who went to Winter Haven to play ball would mind that.

He certainly knew how to run a spring-training camp. Every man was busy every minute, as Williams went back and forth from one field to another, working us all on such fundamentals as sliding and throwing to the cutoff man and backing up bases and all the other necessary, if boring, facets of baseball. Some guys griped, but for my money they had nothing to gripe about. Right from the beginning, the only thing on Williams' mind was to win. He didn't care whether ballplayers liked him or not. All he asked was all they had to give, and he wouldn't settle for less.

"I'm not here to make friends," he used to say. "I'm not in a popularity contest. I want to win and I want a ball club full of other guys who want to win."

The rules he set were reasonable, and I felt we should all obey them. I didn't like the hotel the single men were living in, but it was the team headquarters and I knew everyone would be watching to see what I would do after Carol went home. I could almost hear them saying, "Yaz won't move in. He'll stay where he is. And he and Williams will have a battle about it."

The morning after Carol left, I went up to Williams and said, "Dick, do you want me to move into the hotel?"

"Yes," he said. "I'd appreciate it."

I moved in that night, sacrificing the rest of the rent I had paid on the apartment. And, knowing the press was watching me closely, I continued to do anything that would make it obvious Williams and I were working closely together. I worked hard on the field. I made every exhibition-game trip, never once asking to be excused. Sometimes before a workout Dick would come to me and say, "Yaz, what do you think if we work on the squeeze this morning?" or, "We're going to have sliding practice for a couple of hours." And I would always answer, "Whatever you say, Dick. If you think it will win us a couple of ball games some-where along the line I'm all for it."

I was delighted. For six years all we ever did was go through the motions—get on first base, wait for somebody to hit a home run, do everything the easy way, practice when we felt like it, do nothing when we felt like it. For six years I had seen managers sit back and watch ballplayers do what they pleased while we had one losing season after another. Now at last we had a manager who cared, a manager who wanted to win—in-deed, demanded that we win—a manager who was constantly alert, constantly on the ball, constantly insisting that everyone keep his nose to the grindstone, a manager who wasn't afraid to slap on a heavy fine if necessary, who understood how ballplayers should be handled.

And Williams did understand. He knew Rico Petrocelli's prob-lem was lack of confidence. The Red Sox had brought in Eddie Popowski as a coach because Rico loved the guy and would do anything Pop told him. Williams put Pop's locker next to Rico's so they could talk every day. Pop knew our other kids too, and they all respected him, just as Charlie Schilling and I had when we were kids.

To Williams, each ballplayer was an individual, and he

handled each in just the proper manner. Reggie Smith, a marvelously talented young switch-hitter who could play infield or outfield, needed a prod here and there. When Williams reminded him the Red Sox had an option left on him—meaning they could send him to the minors once more without asking waivers on him—he galvanized Smith into action. Reggie, who had a great year, later said it was the turning point in his career.

Williams set up a weight chart and insisted that every ballplayer stick to it. The guys were expected to report at certain weights and to maintain prescribed weights all season. Joe Foy and George Scott were both benched at one time or another during the season because they ate themselves out of shape. They had to fight to get back into the line-up. So did others who got into Williams' doghouse.

And this was all good. To have a manager that much interested in what was going on, to have a manager who thought only of winning and who wanted nothing more than to keep on winning, to have a manager who cared that much about individuals yet could fuse them all into a team was an experience I hadn't known since playing for Gene Mauch in Minneapolis. Williams, in fact, was much like Mauch—tough and demanding, but not hard to play for if you really wanted to play.

It was worth working hard for a guy like this, and, believe me, I worked. My first spring training under Williams was the toughest I had ever had. After the day's workout I spent an extra half-hour swinging a lead bat, smashing it through a heavy rubber barrier a hundred times, and finished utterly exhausted but feeling wonderful. Nobody else on the club did it that much or at that time, but maybe nobody else appreciated what it meant to have Williams running the team instead of somebody who either wouldn't or couldn't inject a winning spirit into it.

For the fourth year in a row we came up with two fine rookies. In 1964 they were Tony Conigliaro and Dalton Jones, in 1965 Jim Lonborg and Rico Petrocelli, in 1966 George Scott and Joe Foy. The 1967 newcomers were Reggie Smith and Mike Andrews, and they filled two wide-open spots—Smith center field, and Andrews second base. Now we had a young, fast, enthusiastic ball club, with me the dean of the regulars at twenty-seven. Our catching still wasn't strong, and we could have used help with the pitching, but the rest of the team was sound.

So was the manager. He was the key, for he too filled a spot that had been wide open. He said what he pleased, he shocked a few people, he made a few enemies, but he didn't care. All he wanted to do was win. And as we started the 1967 season that was all any of the rest of us wanted to do. Maybe we wouldn't win the pennant, but we wouldn't finish ninth again either. Williams told the press we'd win more games than we'd lose. That would hoist us into the first division, which was all a ninth-place ball club had a right to expect.

Except we expected the moon, and Williams had us reaching for it the day the 1967 season began.

CHAPTER 11

Memories of a Miracle

As long as I live I'll never forget 1967, our miracle year, the year of the underdog, the year of the impossible dream, the year some were kind enough to call the year of the Yaz; yet I can't remember the year in detail, or the things that happened in the order they happened, or exactly when we were up and when we were down. I hit 44 home runs, but I can remember only a few. I knocked in 121 runs, but I can't remember which won ball games or contributed to winning ball games or were driven home in lost causes. I batted .326 and I know I had an unbelievable finish, but I can't remember when I went into the batting lead, or how, or under what conditions. I know we won the pennant, and I can remember all the details of that last two-game series we won against the Twins to clinch it, but the events that led up to that series are a kaleidoscopic jumble in my mind.

The year 1967, the year we won the pennant against odds of 100 to 1, was to me a year of highlights and shadings, of ups and downs, of triumphs and disappointments. We could win a dozen pennants and none will be quite like that one, for it came out of the blue, utterly unexpected, a storybook with a wobbly script and an ending no novelist would dare to invent. It was all too pat—this ninth-place club and this cast of young characters, backed by a few older ones, pulling chestnuts out of fires and dangling on the brink of disaster day after day and week after week.

Here were these four teams fighting for the pennant, not for a day or a week or a month but for nearly half a season, in the wildest battle big-league baseball has ever known. One, Minnesota, a sound ball club only two years away from its last pennant and maybe the favorite to win this one. Another, Detroit, strong all up and down the line, with solid pitching, and maybe co-favorite. A third, Chicago, weak at the plate but with the best pitching in the league and a fighting manager not afraid to take a chance.

And a fourth: Boston—poor little old Boston. A ninth-place team, with one great pitcher and a bunch of brash kids imbued with the spirit of a young manager who laughs at the odds—and with this old-young veteran left fielder with the big long Polish name, who, for reasons he can't explain himself, suddenly can do nothing wrong. How can this upstart team win? What is it doing in this crazy pennant race? Why hasn't it folded long ago? What keeps it alive? And how can anyone in his right mind pick this team to end up ahead of those other three?

How indeed? I know now we were a more solid team than anyone thought. I know now that we were ready, willing, and able to win the pennant nobody thought we could win. I know now that we will win more pennants with much the same team. I know now that nobody panicked, that nobody thought about pressure, that there never was a game we *had* to win that we *didn't* win, that there was always somebody ready to pick up dropped pieces, that we were all heroes.

But I didn't know it while the season was on. I'm not sure any of us, including Dick Williams, knew it. For, like the rest of us, Williams was on a kick, riding on Cloud Nine, giddy with the sweet smell of success, high on a baseball bender that took us all to the very end of the rainbow. I could look back at the records and say, "On this day we did this," or "On that day we did that," but I won't even try. All I want to do now is hit those highlights of memory that will stick in my mind to my dying day. And I want to do it without looking anything up, for I would rather remember them as highlights than as something that must be checked for details.

I remember our first game at Yankee Stadium in New York in mid-April, when a slight black-haired young southpaw named Billy Rohr had a no-hitter going in his first big-league start, with Tommy Tresh leading off the ninth inning for the Yankees. Tresh hit a ball so deep into left I thought it was gone, but I turned around and ran after it anyhow because all I could think of was this boy's no-hitter. The ball stayed in the park, and as it came down I made a desperate leap. It landed in my glove and stuck there as I lost my balance and rolled over in the turf, while off in the distance I could hear people shouting and stamping and clapping and whistling. I may have made better catches, but I don't remember any. The kid lost his no-hitter when Elston Howard singled with two out in the ninth, but he gave the whole ball club a lift and maybe started us on our road to glory.

I remember a day in Chicago when we had a twi-night doubleheader starting at five in the afternoon. On the bus from the hotel I was very nervous, itchy to get started, anxious to know how Gary Peters, the White Sox pitcher in the first game, would try to handle me. It was damp, not a good day for baseball, and the field was a little messy. First time up, Peters threw two breaking balls, and I thought, *He won't try to get me with a fast ball.* I waited for a slider. He threw two more breaking balls, running the count to three and one, then came in with the slider. I hit it to left for a single, and as I was going down the first-base line I thought, *Next time he'll try to get the fast ball by me.* My next time up he threw a slider for a ball, a curve for a strike, then a fast ball which I swung at and missed. *Now another fast ball,* I thought. Peters threw one, and I hit it for a triple to right center. Don McMahon was pitching when I came up for the third time. He had been with the Red Sox, but before that, at Cleveland, he used to throw me sliders low and fast balls away. This time it was a low slider, and I lined it to right for my third hit.

I went to the bat rack to go up for the fourth time in the sixth or seventh inning—we had a big lead—and Dick Williams asked me, "You want to hit, or rest for the second game?"

"I'll hit and then go in," I said.

Wilbur Wood was the Chicago pitcher. He threw the first ball over my head into the screen, and I thought, *Okay, I have three hits. He wants to shake me up a little.* The second pitch was behind me, the third into the screen, the fourth behind me again. Four times in a row he was all over the place, aiming the ball at everything but the plate. I went out for a pinch-runner, and Jim Lonborg, who was pitching, followed me into the locker room.

"Who do you want me to get, Yaz?" he asked. "Name him."

That was Lonborg, ready to fight back with the only weapon he had. And he would fight back for anyone, anyone in a Red Sox uniform, for the Red Sox were his teammates, and when teammates are pulling together on a ball field they're all brothers.

I remember a day in Yankee Stadium when Thad Tillotson, the Yankee pitcher, beaned Joe Foy with a fast ball that bounced high off his helmet. Foy went down, and for an awful moment we thought he had been badly hurt, but he wasn't. Lonborg couldn't wait for Tillotson to come up so he could retaliate. As Tillotson jogged down the first-base line, he said something to Lonny. Then Foy crossed over from third and yelled to Tillotson, "You're not going to do anything. If you're going at him you'll have to get by me first." Then George Scott moved up from first base and the outfielders came in and the two benches emptied, and for a minute everyone just stood around, with nobody doing anything. It didn't look as if anyone would, and I turned to go back to left field.

Just then Joe Pepitone of the Yankees picked up a handful of dirt and playfully threw it at Rico Petrocelli—the two were old pals from Brooklyn—and, as Pepitone took a step toward Rico, Scott grabbed Joe and somebody brought Rico down by the ankles and the whole field was in an uproar. Six or eight guys were in a pile on the ground, and the rest of us were running around, and pretty soon we were pulling guys off the pile, hoping nobody would get spiked. I blindly grabbed somebody, but when he turned around and I saw it was Manager Ralph Houk of the Yankees, one of the toughest guys in baseball, I said to myself, *I want no part of this guy,* and let him go. A great big Yankee kid —must have weighed 230 or so—was sitting on somebody. All I could see were a pair of red socks and a set of spikes sticking out. I pushed the kid far enough off to see it was Conigliaro and thought, *This kid's big enough to handle us both.* Then the boy let Tony up and walked away.

The free-for-all broke up at last. Later Lonny said, "I've got to protect my own ballplayers." That helped to make a real team of us.

I remember a day in June when Conigliaro came up in the eleventh inning with two out and a man on base and the White Sox leading 1–0, at Fenway Park. Conigliaro belted one into the screen at the top of the left-field fence for a two-run homer that won the game. He ran around the bases with his head down, as he often had in the past, but when he looked up after crossing third base, he saw us all waiting for him at the plate. He leaped up and down the rest of the way from third, to be mobbed by the impromptu reception committee. That helped to make a team of us too.

I remember the last game before the All-Star break, in Detroit. We had just lost three in a row to the Tigers, and a couple before that in Los Angeles, to make it five or six in a row. If we lost, all we'd have to think about for four days would be a long losing streak. If we won, we'd have something good to look back on. We won by two or three runs, and I hit a homer off Fred Gladding. And after the All-Star Game we started to roll, winning three in a row from the Orioles and two out of three from the Tigers, who came into town leading the league.

I remember a late-August doubleheader in Yankee Stadium— the Yankees had a bad year, but even so, many of the things I remember came in games with them—when I was in a bad slump. I had won a game the day before with a sacrifice fly, but I couldn't buy a hit. We won the first game of the doubleheader, then lost the second in twenty innings. In the locker room Williams said, "Yaz, come in whenever you want tomorrow. You went twenty-seven innings today, and I think you ought to rest."

I was so wound up I didn't get to sleep until five in the morning, got up at nine-thirty, and by noon was at the ball park, where Buddy LeRoux gave me a long rubdown and I fell asleep. I woke up in the third inning, took a cold shower, got into my uniform, and was on the bench around the sixth or seventh.

"How do you feel?" Williams asked.

"Fine," I said. "I can play."

"Hit for Thomas when he comes up," Williams said.

George Thomas, playing left field, was due to lead off the eighth. Al Downing was pitching, and I went to bat with no hits in my last eighteen times up. *Wait*, I kept saying to myself. *Don't lunge. Hit the fast ball.* Downing came in with a fast ball, and I let it go for a strike; then I fouled off another fast ball. He threw a slider, and I popped it to short right field, but I swung well and I felt good and my confidence was coming back. I trotted down toward third base on the way to left field, and as Joe Foy handed me my glove and cap and sunglasses, which he had brought out from the bench, I said, "I'll get him next time. I feel good. I'm going to hit one out of here."

And in the tenth inning I belted a fast ball into the center-field bleachers—my first hit in nineteen trips—to win the ball game.

I remember Cape Cod Day in Boston. Downing was pitching for the Yankees, and Red Flaherty, who comes from the Cape, was umpiring behind the plate. My first time up, Downing threw a pitch that looked bad to me and Flaherty called it a strike. I was a little irritated, but I didn't say anything. Next time up, Downing threw one high and away and Flaherty called that a strike. Now I was mad. I stepped out of the box, looked around, and said, "Red, you stink. You're calling a lousy game. You're having a lousy day. Bear down behind there."

"Keep it up," Flaherty said, "and you'll be out of the game."

I stepped back in the box and kept it up. I faced the pitcher, and after he threw a called ball I stood there and said, "Boy, Red, you stink. You're brutal. I want to go get sick somewhere you're so bad."

"Keep it up," Flaherty said.

Without looking around, I said, "A lot of your friends from Cape Cod are here. How can you be so bad with all your friends from Cape Cod here?"

"A lot of my neighbors are here too," Flaherty said. "You're trying to show me up in front of them."

Downing was standing on the rubber, getting his sign from the catcher, when, still facing the pitcher, I said, "I'm not trying to show you up, Red. You just stink, that's all."

As Downing began his stretch, Flaherty stepped away, called time, pointed at me, and said, "You're out of there."

I turned around and yelled, "What are you throwing me out for? I didn't use any bad language." The fans started booing while Flaherty pointed to the dugout, and as I walked away I said, "Red, not only do I think you stink, but I think all your neighbors from Cape Cod think you stink too."

It was the only time all year I got thrown out of a game.

I remember a June day in Chicago when Manager Eddie Stanky of the White Sox said I was an all-star from the neck down. I was annoyed at first, but the next day I went 6 for 9 as we split a doubleheader. I hit a home run my last time up, and as I approached third base I tipped my cap to Stanky in the White Sox dugout.

I remember a night in Washington I was supposed to take off because Dick Williams thought I could use a rest. But I felt so good he let me play, and I hit a home run off Bob Priddy my first time up. By the fifth inning we had a good lead with another rally going, and I was due to come up soon.

"Hey, Yaz," Russ Gibson yelled, "Joe Coleman, Jr.'s warming up."

The last time I had faced Joe Coleman, Jr., he struck me out twice. Now everybody on the bench started laughing, and Williams said, "You've had enough, Yaz. Go ahead in and take half a day off anyhow."

"Not until I face Joe Coleman, Jr.," I said. "How do you suppose he struck me out twice in a row? Why, I hit home runs off his dad all the time in batting practice."

"Well," said Gibson, "he's all heated up for you, Yaz. Here he comes."

Everybody was still laughing and kidding about those strikeouts when I went up to bat. As I approached the plate I thought, *He got me on fast balls. That's what he'll throw now.* By this time all the Red Sox players were on the top step of the dugout, yelling and clapping and laughing, while I moved into the batter's box, waiting for the fast ball. Sure enough, in it came, and I belted it out of the park. And when I got back to the bench Gibby said, "That'll teach Joe Coleman, Jr., to mess around with you."

I remember the California Angels coming into Boston about three games out of the lead and in the middle of a winning streak. We beat them the first game of the series; then they took an 8–0 lead in the second. Reggie Smith hit a home run to make it 8–1 and start us rolling. We caught them finally, and Jerry Adair hit a homer in the ninth to beat them. Afterward Manager Bill Rigney of the Angels said, "Yesterday you broke my winning streak. Today you broke my heart."

I remember when Adair came over to us in June from the White Sox in a trade for Don McMahon. At the time the White Sox were five games in front, and somebody said, "Poor Adair. He started last year with Baltimore, and they won the pennant after he was traded to the White Sox. He starts this year with the White Sox, and now that they're way ahead he gets traded to the Red Sox." When we won the pennant Adair said, "Getting cheated out of one pennant was bad enough. Two in a row would have been too much."

I remember Elston Howard, after we got him from the Yankees, leaping high to catch a throw from José Tartabull in right field, then coming down and tagging Ken Berry at the plate to complete a double play in the last of the ninth in Chicago. That ended the ball game, a real squeaker because Berry represented the tying run.

I remember tying another squeaker, this time in Detroit, with a home run in the ninth, and Dalton Jones winning it with another homer in the tenth. We won so many games like that, with first one guy, then another coming up with key hits in clutches.

I don't remember the details of that crazy four-team pennant race, but I do remember one day when we were all just about as close as you can get. The Twins and the White Sox were tied for the league lead, while we and the Tigers were only one percentage point behind. That was the closest the four clubs got, and after that we never fell more than two games behind.

I remember daily baseball discussions with Carol in that wild month of September. Up to then she had been just an ordinary fan, but as the end of the season approached, with us still in the thick of the fight, she became more and more emotionally involved. Every day the discussion began the same way. When I came down to breakfast she said, "Do you think we'll win the pennant?" And I said, "Yes, we've got a chance."

Each day the talk depended on what had happened the day before. Once I said, "Chicago's folding. That's one team eliminated." Two days later the White Sox were right back in the race. After that I never predicted that any team would fold, because you couldn't count any of us out as long as there was a mathematical chance.

Carol went to every home game the last month of the season. One night she went down for a hot dog in the fourth inning and I hit a home run while she was underneath the stands. She stayed there for the rest of the game, and from then on she always went under the stands in the fourth inning and waited until the game was over. In the last ten days of the season she didn't see a game beyond the fourth inning.

After we lost two to Cleveland in the last week of the season, I thought we were dead. We had two games left, with Minnesota; the Tigers had four with California; and the White Sox had their two best pitchers, Gary Peters and Joel Horlen, ready for a twi-night doubleheader at Kansas City.

"We're all done," I told Carol the night we lost the second Cleveland game. "California will at least split with the Tigers, and Chicago will take two from the Athletics tonight and back in. I hate to see it end that way, but I'm afraid that's how it will be."

That night I called the Boston papers every half-hour for the score of that doubleheader in Kansas City. The Athletics astounded everyone by beating Peters in the first game, and Carol said, "What do you think now?"

"It's a little better," I said. "But Horlen will win the second game, of course."

Only Horlen didn't win the second game. The Athletics beat him too, to sweep the doubleheader and practically knock the White Sox out of the pennant race. They were eliminated two days later.

I remember my parents telling me how they drove the five miles from Bridgehampton to the beach at Noyack every day to listen to Red Sox ball games from a station in Connecticut, across Long Island Sound. It was right in the middle of potato-harvesting time when the season ended, but they drove to Boston Saturday for the Minnesota series and drove home Sunday night. During the two ball games with the Twins they took turns keeping Carol company under the stands when she went down there after the fourth inning.

I remember people asking me about pressure all the time, and if I felt it and how I stood it. I was riding too high to feel pressure, on that same kick we all were on, living in a dream world full of heroics and victories, going about in a sort of baseball trance, looking forward to every game, sure we would make it when nobody else took a commanding lead, for we were a team of destiny and I was a man of destiny. I was so sure of this that I wasn't even aware of pressure.

I remember saying to Carol once, "If we sat down every day and planned situations in which I could be the hero, at bat and on the field, we couldn't have come closer than what actually happened." And that's the way it was—the base hit, the home run, the great catch, the sure throw, all made to order for me, needing only the execution on my part.

I remember anticipating situations, then seeing them develop. In Baltimore once we were down 5–4, with the ninth man up and me not due for three more. Tom Phoebus was pitching for the Orioles and he had handcuffed me the first part of the game. Both times up, I had felt lousy. My timing was off, my swing wasn't right, there was a deadness I couldn't seem to shake. Suddenly I felt wonderful and I thought, *I'm coming up there with a man on base and the Orioles leading 5–4, and I'm going to hit a home run to put us in front.* Then I was in the on-deck circle when Jerry Adair singled with two out, and I came up so sure I would hit a home run that I would have been disappointed if I hadn't. But I knew it, I *knew* I'd hit one. The count went to two balls and no strikes, Phoebus came in with a fast ball, and I drove it out of the park to put us ahead.

I remember my dad objecting when I started going for home runs. "Never mind the home runs," he said. "Get the base hits and win the batting title."

Frank Robinson of the Orioles was way ahead of me in batting at the time, and I said, "I don't have a shot at the batting title, Dad. I want home runs now."

Then Robinson got hurt, came back with impaired vision, and slumped, while I got hot. I caught him and hit home runs too.

I remember an amazing streak of runs I drove in that clinched the RBI title for me. One week Harmon Killebrew and I were even, and the next I was miles ahead of him. Before I was through I drove in something like 20 runs in 15 games. But we stayed close in home runs, and when the Twins came in for that last weekend series we each had 43.

I remember my 44th and his 44th, both in the Saturday game, and the events that led up to them. Jim Kaat started for the Twins, and he was tough, although I hit a curve ball for a single my first time up. But you can't hit Kaat for distance when he has his stuff and control, and he had both that day. Then he hurt his arm in the third inning and had to leave the game. We were glad to see him go, although we got no bargain in Jim Perry, who took his place. Perry was tough too, but we figured we were due to beat him.

The first time I faced Perry we had a man on second with two outs and the Twins leading 1–0. I missed a fast ball, took a couple of pitches, took a slider for a strike, got the count up to three and two, then struck out swinging at a slider outside and up a little. I was looking for the break, and the ball didn't break. Actually, even though I struck out, I wasn't unhappy. Perry didn't have real good stuff, and I had taken a good cut at the ball and knew I was in the groove.

In the fifth, Reggie Smith doubled and Dalton Jones and Jerry Adair each singled, to make it 1–1 when I came up with two out and men on first and third. Once again the count went to three and two, with Perry mixing sliders and fast balls. His fast ball wasn't live and he had to get the next pitch over the plate, so I looked for a slider, got one, and hit it to right center for a single that scored Jones and gave us a 2–1 lead. The Twins tied it again in the sixth. Then George Scott hit a home run in our half to put us ahead, 3–2.

When I came up in the seventh, Andrews and Adair were on base and Jim Merritt was pitching. While watching him from the on-deck circle I thought, *He throws me a lot of sliders in Minneapolis because of that short right field out there, but it's long in right here and he might try a fast ball. But he'd rather throw me sliders.* And I went to the plate looking for the slider, but with the fast ball in the back of my mind.

His first pitch was a fast ball, high and straight. When it didn't sink at all, I knew his fast ball wasn't moving and I could hit it out of there. He missed with a slider on his next pitch, making it two balls and no strikes, then threw a good slider, which I took for a strike. When he missed with another slider to make the count three and one, I knew he had to come in with the fast ball, that he would throw it high, and that it wouldn't sink. He wasn't fast or sneaky or the least bit deceptive, and I remember thinking, *Flip the bat—make sure to get out front—make sure to stay on top of the ball—don't go into a crouch and try to swing too hard—get on top—get out front—flick the wrist . . .*

The pitch came in, and I didn't really crack it, like some of my home runs, but met it just the way I wanted to. The minute the ball left my bat, I knew it was gone for homer number 44. It went straight out and a little to the right, into the bleachers, to give us a 6–2 lead and put me one ahead of Killebrew.

Gary Bell, who had relieved José Santiago, was pitching for us in the ninth. Cesar Tovar hit a double, and when Killebrew came up, Bell missed with his first pitch. Dick Williams stopped the game to talk to Bell, and I thought, *He's telling Bell to get the ball over the plate so they won't have two on with Oliva and Allison coming up. And the way Killebrew's been hitting, he'll murder it.* Williams went back to the dugout, Bell threw a fast ball right down the pipe, and Killebrew hit into the left-field screen for his 44th.

Although a little irritated that I'd have to share the home-run title, or maybe lose it the next day if Killebrew hit one and I didn't, I realized that this was good strategy. Killebrew's homer didn't hurt us, because it left us still two runs ahead with the bases empty. But if Killebrew had walked and Oliva had belted one with two on, it would have made the score 6–5 with the Twins rolling, and no telling what might have happened. This way, the home run cut them off, and the game ended at 6–4.

The minute we got into the locker room, Williams said, "Don't be mad at Bell or Howard. I called that pitch."

"I know you did, Dick," I said. "I figured you were telling Bell to throw the fast ball and get it over the plate. You didn't want to walk the man."

And still later, when I left the locker room to meet Carol, Dick came out and said to her, "I'm sorry about that pitch Bell threw. I called it."

There wasn't any reason to apologize. The maneuver was simply another of the dozens of things that gave us the pennant. And if I have my choice between a pennant and a triple crown, I'll take the pennant every time.

CHAPTER 12

My First World Series

The World Series was an anticlimax. After the frenetic finish of the pennant race we were all emotionally drained. Yet we obviously had something left, because we forced the Cardinals to seven games and lost to them only because Jim Lonborg couldn't get as much rest as Bob Gibson. Even though Gibson, a great pitcher, beat us three times, I think we could have won the first game. If we had, we would have won the series in six games and there wouldn't have been any seventh.

It's pretty hard to get charged up, even for a World Series, after reaching the emotional peaks we hit in the pennant race. The highest peak of all came in the last weekend of the season, when we beat the Twins twice in a row to clinch the pennant, after they had come into Boston a game ahead of us. Still, I sometimes think we would have been better off if the World Series had started the next day. We were hot and we might have stayed hot. Instead, we had a two-day layoff at the wrong time. Two days off when you're in a slump is fine. But when you're in a hot streak you don't even want one day off.

I was so tired and let down that on Monday I didn't even think about the World Series. Carol and I slept at the Colonial Inn on Sunday night, then went home, where all I did was lie around the house, read the papers, and talk to the landscape man who was going to put left field into my back yard. At the end of every season the Red Sox get rid of the outfield turf, because they grow new turf each season. When the Fenway Park groundskeeper told me this, I asked if I could have some.

"After the World Series," he said, "we'll roll up left field and ship it out to your house."

We had a noon workout Tuesday, but the weather wasn't good and we couldn't get anywhere near enough batting practice. That night Carol and I went back to the Colonial Inn. I drove to the ball park early Wednesday for the first game of the series. But I still wasn't high, still didn't have that wonderful feeling of exhilaration, that tremendous eagerness to play ball, that superman attitude which gave me the conviction that whatever had to be done to win in the clutch I could do. I just felt blah. The big job was done: we had won the pennant. How could we get excited about the World Series?

Except that I was annoyed at the Cardinals. They talked as if we didn't belong on the same field with them. They knew we were hurting at the plate without Tony Conigliaro, and they said that would make the job easier for them. So actually my first spark of real desire came from the Cardinals themselves. If they hadn't talked so uppity—and acted that way too—they might have had an easier time with us.

For we weren't ready for that first game. We were still in a fog from the regular season, still looking back on what we had done instead of looking forward to what we had to do. And now, after two days off, we were rusty. Tuesday's practice hadn't been long enough. I looked forward to batting practice Wednesday before the game, because our timing was off and we needed work to sharpen it up.

We didn't get it because somebody messed up the pre-game schedule. Instead of forty-five minutes of batting practice, we only got twenty. In twenty minutes a ball club can't possibly get enough batting practice after a two-day layoff. I can't speak for the others, but I was still cold and my timing wasn't right because I couldn't take enough swings. Normally I take about twenty, but this time I had only six or seven. I knew before I left the batting cage that I wasn't ready.

Gibson later pitched two great games, but he wasn't nearly as good in that first one. He threw me a couple of pitches I should have creamed. One was in the fourth inning, when he hung a slider. I should have belted it into right field somewhere, but I bounced out to second because I didn't hit it squarely. In the ninth I flied to left on an outside pitch I should have hit hard enough to reach or clear the wall there. My timing was off, and my reflexes weren't right. I simply hadn't had enough work.

I went 0 for 4, and we lost a 2–1 game I'm sure we would have won if we hadn't been short-changed on batting practice. José Santiago started for us because Lonborg, who must have three days' rest to be effective, had beaten the Twins the previous Sunday. Santiago was in trouble all afternoon, but he did a magnificent job getting out of it. The Cardinals scored both their runs on infield outs by Roger Maris. Our lone run came when Santiago himself banged a home run into the nets in left center in the third inning.

After Gibson got me in the fourth inning, I asked Fitzie to call the ground crew and tell them I was going to take batting practice later. I would have done it even if I had got hits my next two times up. Joe Foy agreed to pitch to me, and after I had talked to the writers in the locker room and given the fans time to leave, I got back into uniform, grabbed a couple of bats, and started for the field. Rico Petrocelli, who had struck out three times, asked where I was going, and when I said, "Out to hit," he said, "Mind if I come along?" Ken Harrelson—he'd gone 0 for 3—also joined us.

The workout lasted about an hour and a half, with all of us— Foy, Petrocelli, Harrelson, and me—taking turns pitching and batting. After forty-five minutes of hitting, my timing was back, my swing was good, and everything was fine. I got so sharp that I hit six Foy pitches in a row into the right-field bullpen or stands with just a flick of the wrists, and when I came in I said to Jerry Buckley, the Red Sox photographer, "I'm going to hit a couple out tomorrow." I was only half kidding.

The writers, who were in from all over the country, made a big deal out of that workout, because I guess it was the first time they had ever seen ballplayers take batting practice after a World Series game, but I didn't think anything of it. Whenever my timing is off in a ball game, I take batting practice later if we're not leaving town right away. Besides, my pride was hurt. The World Series is baseball's greatest showcase, and I wanted to make the kind of showing that would prove the American League is as good as the National League. I particularly wanted to give the Cardinals a run for their money, because they thought they were going to win the thing in four straight. With enough batting practice that first day, we'd have beaten them in six; and if Conigliaro could have played, I think we'd have done it in five. Gibson would have lost the first game and won the fourth, and wouldn't have had another chance to pitch.

Every time I faced Hughes in the second game, I was going for a home run. That was the day Lonny, who pitched a one-hitter, had a perfect game until he walked Curt Flood with one out in the seventh, and a no-hitter until Julian Javier doubled with two out in the eighth. Hughes walked me the first time I faced him, after I hit a good slider out of the park foul by a few feet. He's a fast-ball pitcher, and I guess I shook him up a little with that long foul, because all I saw from him were fast balls after that. And that was all I wanted to see. I love a pitcher who throws high and straight and tries to blow the ball by me.

When I led off in the fourth inning—nobody had scored yet—the count had gone to two balls and a strike when Hughes threw me a fast ball over the middle of the plate between the knees and the belt. It was a pretty good pitch, but my timing was perfect and I put it into the right-field seats, a line drive I hit with a flick of my wrists. He kept the ball away from me in the sixth, when I flied to left, and that was the last I saw of Hughes that day.

I came up in the seventh with two on, nobody out, the Red Sox leading 2–0, and Joe Hoerner pitching for the Cardinals in relief of Ron Willis. When Frank Malzone gave me his scouting report on Hoerner he said, "You don't have to look for his breaking ball. He jams left-handed hitters, tries to throw the ball by them, throws hard, has a good sinker." I went up guessing a fast ball, and Hoerner threw me one after another. The first pitch tailed in on me and I missed it, but my swing was good, just a fraction late. After missing twice on the outside, Hoerner put one down the middle which I should have murdered, but I fouled it back, to run the count to two and two. When he missed low and away, it was three and two, and I knew he would come in on me fast and tight—like the first pitch. *I know it's coming in,* I thought. *I know it's going to be up. The thing is not to try to swing too hard.* The pitch came in exactly where I expected it. I stuck the bat out in front, a nice quick swing, and hit a real shot, a long high belt that landed ten rows up in the right-field stands. With Jack Lamabe pitching in the eighth, I hit a single to center for a perfect day at bat, 3 for 3. That was a curve ball, low and in.

We flew to St. Louis after the game and the next day worked out in dismal weather. I hit quite a bit, because the background at Busch Memorial Stadium isn't too good and I wanted to get used to it. The weather was better for the third game. After I got into uniform I took about fifteen swings, then, to loosen up, worked out at third base a while.

First time up, Nelson Briles, the Cardinal pitcher, hit me in the calf of the leg, and I was mad. I felt he tried to hit me because of those two home runs in Boston, and I wanted our pitcher to brush back the first guy who batted for them. But Dick Williams came out of the dugout protesting, and the umpire got him and Manager Red Schoendienst together and warned them, "No more throwing at each other." That robbed us of our only weapon of retaliation. Briles is nowhere near the pitcher Gibson is, but he eliminated me as a factor. I was so sore I kept trying to pull the ball instead of hitting it down the middle, and I grounded out to second three times. We lost the game, 3–2.

Gibson shut us out in the fourth game, giving up only five hits. I got two of them, a single off his curve in the first inning and a double to center off his fast ball in the ninth. But we were never in the game, because the Cardinals collected four runs in the first inning, and it's a rare day when you can spot Gibson four runs and catch him in his own ball park.

With the Cardinals leading us three games to one, they were so cocky they didn't even take their luggage to the ball park before the fifth game, expecting they'd end the series then and not have to go back to Boston. But that didn't make us half so mad as a column by Jim Murray calling us the "Dead Sox," which infuriated everyone. Dick Williams quoted the column in his pre-game locker-room talk, then put it on the bulletin board. To add to our annoyance, Carol and a couple of other Red Sox wives had been upstaged by some of the wives of Cardinal ballplayers when they went into a room set aside for the girls at Busch Stadium. The only member of the Cardinal party who showed any real class was Stan Musial, who was a gentleman all the way through, never popped off in the newspapers or anywhere else, and was always pleasant.

One thing we knew: whatever the Cardinals might have thought, they were going to have to win this series in Boston. Lonborg made sure of that with his three-hitter in the fifth game. All I did that day was hit a double off Ray Washburn in the eighth which didn't figure in the scoring. But we won, and that was what counted. And the Cardinals had to go home for their luggage to make the trip to Boston.

The sixth game was a ball. Dick Williams started Gary Waslewski, and the kid did a great job for five-plus innings, while the rest of us murdered Cardinal pitching. Rico Petrocelli hit homers his first two times up, the second one in the fourth inning. Reggie

Smith and I also had homers in the fourth, which broke a World Series record—three in one inning. I also had a couple of singles, and when we won we forced the series to its seven-game limit.

I guess Williams will hear about that seventh game for the rest of his life, but he didn't do anything I wouldn't have done. He caught a lot of criticism for starting Lonborg with only two days' rest, but Lonny was our strength, and it was, after all, the last game of the year. He didn't have it—just ran out of gas—but I don't think I'd have taken him out any sooner than Dick did. When Dick went out to talk to him in the sixth inning, with Javier up, nobody out, and two men on base, a good many observers thought he should have yanked Lonny, but I didn't. Javier isn't a power hitter, and the last thing you'd expect from him was the home run he delivered. Lonborg finished the inning and went out with dignity. Gibson beat us for his third win of the series, but none of us had anything to be ashamed of. To start a season 100-to-1 underdogs and to end it carrying the World Series to seven games against a club everyone thought would kill us is hardly a disgrace. Manager Red Schoendienst of the Cardinals took much of the bitterness away for me when we met in the players' parking lot after the last game. He shook hands and said, "It was a great series, Yaz, and you're a great ballplayer."

With the season over, I hit the jackpot, starting with the Most Valuable Player award. There was a slightly sour note when a Minnesota writer voted for Cesar Tovar of the Twins, which kept me from winning unanimously, but of course that was the guy's privilege and, whether I liked it or not, I had to respect his right to exercise it. Without taking anything away from Tovar, who had a fine season and played several different positions with distinction (as did our own Jerry Adair), I would have felt better if the writer had given his vote to Harmon Killebrew. For my money, he, not Tovar, was the Twins' most valuable player.

I was invited to appear on a number of television shows, including the Match Game, Johnny Carson, and Merv Griffin. Invitations flooded in for banquets and special occasions all over the country, and I won awards in dozens of cities—the Sid Mercer in New York, the Dapper Dan in Pittsburgh, the Sultan of Swat in Baltimore, the Sam Rice in Washington, the Ty Cobb in Atlanta, the Triple Crown and Most Valuable Player in Boston, and many others.

My biggest thrill was a visit to the White House on January 23, where Norma and Dick Williams, Joe DiMaggio, and Carol and I met President Lyndon B. Johnson. I asked him to accept a Grecian urn which I won as the Athlete-of-the-Year. It was one of four awards I gave away. The one which I most wanted to win was the $10,000 Hickok Belt, which goes each year to the Professional Athlete-of-the-Year and is not announced until late January. After I won it and went to Rochester, New York, to accept it, I had my picture taken with my biggest grin. During the summer of 1968 I will give that to a man I deeply admire and to whom I owe a great debt of gratitude.

Because President John F. Kennedy was my idol, I gave my Sultan of Swat award to his brother, Senator Edward M. (Ted) Kennedy of Massachusetts. It is now on display in the Senator's Boston office. And I gave my Sid Mercer award to Anthony P. DeFalco, Massachusetts Commissioner of Administration.

Tony DeFalco is a very special friend, a wonderful guy, for whom I have both affection and respect. As Governor Volpe's right-hand man, he is one of the busiest people in Massachusetts, but he has always had time for his friends. Before he was Commissioner of Administration and while I was still struggling for the recognition that finally came to me in 1967, he and I were as close as we are today. We are both deeply interested in handicapped children, and in fact Tony was given special recognition in the winter of 1967 by the Massachusetts Association for Retarded Children. Through him, I was chairman of the organization's 1967–1968 fund drive. At present I am also co-chairman of the Jimmy Fund, which helps to raise money for research in children's cancer.

YAZ

I think the things adults do can and should serve as an inspiration to children, and I hope the breaks I have had will remind kids who have followed my career of the opportunities that still exist for anyone willing to work for them. Up to the time I began playing professional baseball, I did not have things easy. Everyone in my family had to work hard for what we earned, and my brother and I were brought up to appreciate the fruits of hard work.

They came to me in huge chunks, far beyond my wildest dreams, but I feel I earned them. I think any youngster with determination, the ability to concentrate, and the willingness to work can be successful in anything he tries. My goal was success in baseball, but it could have been any other sport, or any business, for that matter. Determination, concentration, and hard work can help overcome almost any obstacle. During the winter I do a good deal of public speaking, much of it before children, and that is the message I try hardest to put across to them.

One of my toughest decisions in the winter of 1967–1968 was what to do and what not to do. After that fantastic baseball season, the demands on my time were tremendous. With the help of my business manager, Larry Polans, I screened out all invitations to appear except those that were essential. At the same time, I provided for a future in business by signing a long-term contract with an investment firm.

Any time I feel I'm something pretty special, in view of all the honors that came my way, I think of a trip I made to Miami Beach with Larry Polans and a couple of other fellows a week or ten days after the World Series. With hundreds of people checking in for a convention, the hotel lobby was mobbed. When we finally worked our way to the desk, one of the guys said confidently, "Is Mr. Carl Yastrzemski's room ready?"

"Does he have a reservation?" the clerk demanded.

Half an hour later, when I finally got my key, I went up in the elevator with my ears burning from the ribbing I was getting from my colleagues. But when we reached the room I felt better because a vase of flowers and a basket of fruit with a card were on the dresser.

"See," I said triumphantly, "they *do* know me around here."

"What does the card say?" somebody asked.

I picked it up and read aloud: "Welcome, Charles Yastrzemski."

To this day those guys call me "Charles."